Options Trading for Beginners

How to Crash the Market and Make Profit with Stocks and Options Day Trading Strategies for a Living

By

Simon Jordan

© **Copyright 2020 by Simon Jordan - All rights reserved.**

This document is geared towards providing exact and reliable information in regards to the topic and issue covered. The publication is sold with the idea that the publisher is not required to render accounting, officially permitted, or otherwise, qualified services. If advice is necessary, legal or professional, a practiced individual in the profession should be ordered.

- From a Declaration of Principles which was accepted and approved equally by a Committee of the American Bar Association and a Committee of Publishers and Associations.

In no way is it legal to reproduce, duplicate, or transmit any part of this document in either electronic means or in printed format. Recording of this publication is strictly prohibited and any storage of this document is not allowed unless with written permission from the publisher. All rights reserved.

The information provided herein is stated to be truthful and consistent, in that any liability, in terms of inattention or otherwise, by any usage or abuse of any policies, processes, or directions contained within is the solitary and utter responsibility of the recipient reader. Under no circumstances will any legal responsibility or blame be held against the publisher for any reparation, damages, or monetary loss due to the information herein, either directly or indirectly.

Respective authors own all copyrights not held by the publisher.

The information herein is offered for informational purposes solely, and is universal as so. The presentation of the information is without contract or any type of guarantee assurance.

The trademarks that are used are without any consent, and the publication of the trademark is without permission or backing by the trademark owner. All trademarks and brands within this book are for clarifying purposes only and are the owned by the owners themselves, not affiliated with this document.

Table Of Contents

INTRODUCTION 7

CHAPTER 1: OPTIONS TRADING - THE BASICS 9

1.1 What are Options? 9

1.2 Options Contracts in the Stock Market 13

1.3 Stocks Trading Vs. Options Trading 15

1.4 The Options Jargons 18

1.5 Calculating the Margin in Options Trading 22

CHAPTER 2: TYPES, STYLES, PROS, AND CONS OF OPTIONS TRADING 25

2.1 Types and Styles of Options 25

2.2 The Pricing Mechanism 31

2.3 The Pros of options trading 37

2.4 The cons of options trading 39

CHAPTER 3: OPTIONS TRADING AND RISK MANAGEMENT 41

3.1 Delta (D) 41

3.2 Gamma (G) 44

3.3 Theta (Q) 45

3.4 Vega (n) 46

3.5 Rho (r) 47

CHAPTER 4: GETTING DEEPER INTO THE OPTIONS PRICING 49

4.1 Moving Averages 49

4.2 The Momentum 53

4.3 Support and Resistance 57

4.4 Trend Lines 62

4.5 Candlestick Analysis 65

4.6 Benefits and Importance of Technical Analysis 66

CHAPTER 5: STRATEGIES FOR OPTIONS TRADING 69

5.1 Long Call/ Long Put (Going Long Strategies) 69

5.2 Long/Short (Strangles and Straddles) 71

5.3 Iron Condor 73

5.4 Iron Butterfly 73

5.5 Equity Collar 74

5.6 Short Gut 75

5.7 Long Gut 77

CHAPTER 6: SETTING UP FOR THE ULTIMATE SUCCESS 78

6.1 The Trader's Mindset 78

6.2 Keeping a Trading Journal 79

6.3 Buying and Selling Calls as a Learning Opportunity 81

6.4 Types of Trading 83

6.5 Risk Management 86

CONCLUSION 89

Introduction

Individuals compromise options to benefit value proceeds onward the financial exchange. That is, brokers utilize the strategy for purchasing low and offering high to make benefits from trades.

Options are useful assets in the money related world. They give the holders the right, however not the commitment, to purchase or sell an advantage later on at a cost decided today. They are utilized as protection and as a wellspring of theoretical benefits. The worth is gotten from the estimation of an essential resource or security. However, it isn't indistinguishable from the evaluation of that benefit or protection.

You can purchase options that terminate at different dates later on. The more significant part of the activity is fixated on options that lapse inside seven days to a month, yet a few options terminate a little while, months, and even a very long time into what's to come. As we'll see, the lapse date for the choice is something you'll have to give close consideration to.

In any case, for little financial specialists, probably the best thing about options is the exceptional yield on venture or ROI!

So options exchanging is increasingly open that day or swing trading stocks as a result of the low capital sums required to begin, and you'll procure a lot higher ROI!

Being fruitful in exchanging requires exhausting work and a ton of contemplating, and this idea applies not exclusively to choose transferring yet to every money-related activity of this sort. Be careful about time scales in options exchanging. Recall that in the initial hardly any days or half a month, you won't perceive any sensational movements in the estimation of your options.

The explanation behind this is the way that the exchanging benefit originates from the loss of different merchants. The method of getting benefits is similar to whether you exchange subsidiaries, offers, or options. The measure of cash that goes around is littler when you decrease the commissions that vendors and intermediaries take. These measures of money are one reason why numerous dealers lose during the exchange. You ought to teach yourself to keep away from the destiny of a large portion of these agents. Figure out how to exchange all the more astutely, as it will assist you with flourishing or, at the very least, to make due in the exchanging market. Consider these next pages just as the beginning of your options exchanging venture. You will have the option to perceive and characterize the essential terms and systems for your future profession. It should give you the establishment that you require and rouse you to look advance and instruct yourself further.

I trust you are as excited about exchanging options as I am. We should feel free to begin!

Chapter 1: Options Trading - The Basics

Trading options are just like buying and selling stocks; however, massive versions do exist. Unlike stocks, there are varieties of options (calls and puts), which can be contracts that deliver the proprietor the strength to shop for or promote underlying safety like a stock. However, like stocks, options are traded on alternate option platforms, and individual buyers can function shopping for and promoting orders through a brokerage firm.

The buying and selling of the options aren't always new. Indeed in 1973, the primary options contract indexed made its debut at the Chicago Board Options Exchange. Although an option nowadays is incredibly near what it became then, a great deal has changed. The maximum giant distinction is the market's complexity, in phrases of creditors, exchanged contracts, and exchange rates. This has advanced exponentially, and extra trading options for people are to be had now than ever before.

Investors are the use of options for numerous purposes. A name option is, in particular, a settlement that offers the bearer the proper to shop for a stock for a particular duration at a hard and fast rate. Some investors buy calls after they foresee an extra extensive alternate in the percentage rate. Others can promote calls after they anticipate a stock rate to flat-trade or pass lower.

1.1 What are Options?

Options are contracts that grant a bearer the proper, however not the duty, to either sell or purchase options or stocks of any underlying asset at a preset value at or before any contract expires. Options could also be purchased through mutual investment accounts, like all different quality categories.

Options square measure very powerful as they will improve the portfolio of a personal. They are doing this by adding financial gain, providing leverage, and even protection. Reckoning on the case, there's normally a state of affairs of options suited to the goal of an investor. To limit drawback losses, a simplified example would be to use choices as an efficient hedge against a declining stock exchange. Also, options will be accustomed to generate revenue or revenues. Also, they're oft used for theoretical functions, like wagering on stock direction.

An option could be a contract between a buyer and a marketer regarding a specific stock or different investment. The option client has the correct to force the option marketer to try and do regardless of the contract specifies inside the time-limit set by the deal. Once the client has exercised the option, the vendor should follow the option's directions.

The options belong to the broader securities cluster called derivatives. The value of a by-product depends on or springs from the price of one thing else. As an example, wine is grape-oriented juice, which could be a tomato by-product, and an option could be a stock by-product. Options are specific derivatives of monetary securities — their worth depends on the value of another quality. Samples of derivatives embody calls, puts, futures, forwards, swaps, and mortgage-backed securities, among others.

Investors want brokerage accounts to take a position within the stocks that they hope can rework their initial investments into a life-changing material resource.

However, it's crucial to decide on a broker that provides you access to any or all the various styles of investments that square measure vital to you.

Whereas most brokers can meet basic desires, UN agencies need to require advantage of subtle investment ways need to use caution to pick out brokers who will give them the chance to trade and also the resources needed to form the correct choices in those areas.

Stock options are not as difficult as individuals would build them appear. Typically individuals ask to form them look difficult. However, it's a straightforward issue that just about everybody will perceive. Don't discourage, as a novice, into feeling that commercialism options are a difficult investment. You will be afraid, however straightforward it's, and surprise why you've got never sooner invested within it. There are four concerns that the investors would need to take into account once collaborating available choices. Bringing these concerns under consideration would have a positive result on their commerce.

One way to intensify the commercialism game is to seem at the options market. Options commercialism could be a ton completely different from marketing stocks or mutual funds; however, it will accompany some real edges for investors too. Here, you will take a glance at what options commercialism is expressly and the way it will assist you.

The most critical point of a possibility is that the client of the option has the right to exercise the contract, as its name suggests, however, is beneath no obligation to try and do, therefore. The options client can, therefore, solely use this right once it's informed do, therefore. Within the following example, say the call possibility has allowed the client to pay $100 per share for a particular stock.

If the stock is listed within the open marketplace for $50 per share, the option client will not exercise the options, because it would be stupid to pay $100 on the free market below the chance for a share, the customer, or the client might buy for $50.

However, if the market share value were $175, then the client would exercise the correct, as $100 would be a bargain, or a discount, or cut value over the prevailing share price.

Let me say, a call possibility on a given stock offers the client select the proper to get a precise variety of shares at any time before a mere expiration date at a given value. If the client exercises the correct, the option vender should sell the stock to the option client.

Put options, on the contrary, offer the client option the right to sell stock at a given value, therefore shielding the client possibility from losses within the stock.

You may additionally mix completely different decision and place options to require advantage of a lot of advanced options approaches that may build a profit in a very range of circumstances.

In recent years Stock options (contracts that provide a capitalist the right to sell or purchase a stock at a given value and date) were a topic of concern. We have a tendency to see a lot of folks obtaining curious about trading options. The worth of stock choices has contributed to an excessive amount of discussion. Several say it is a scam; some say it is not a worthy investment, whereas others say they are minting millions out of it. Now, these speculations lead us in one direction, namely: knowing what stock options are. To answer this question accurately, we have a tendency to aim to have to be compelled to re-evaluate stock options terribly fastidiously and apprehend everything concerning them. This data makes it easier to form selections with real proof, instead of exploitation hypothesis. Having expertise provides you an additional advantage and places you in a very sturdy position.

As a novice merchant, information gathering will amendment your mercantilism skills.

Obtaining the requisite skills and information among a matter of your time would cause you to a skilled within the trade.

Apart from getting information, learning to use is important. This may mean doing what you have got learned virtually. Many folks get data; however, many are unable to form effective use of it for their own betterment.

1.2 Options Contracts in the Stock Market

Options Contract

An options contract is an understanding between a purchaser and dealer that gives the buyer of choice the option to purchase or sell a specific resource sometime in the future at a settled upon cost. Options contracts are regularly utilized in protections, products, and land exchanges.

Working Algorithm of an Options Contract

There are a few sorts of options contracts in budgetary exchanges. A trade exchanged choice, for instance, is a formalized agreement that is settled through a clearinghouse and is ensured. These trade exchanged options spread investment opportunities, item options, security and loan fee options, file options, and prospects options. Another sort of options contract is an over-the-counter alternative, which is an exchange between two private gatherings. This may incorporate loan cost options, cash conversion standard options, and trades (for example, exchanging long and short terms loan costs).

The fundamental highlights of trade exchanged alternative, for example, a call options contract gives an option to purchase 100 portions of a security at a given cost by a set date. The options contract charges a market-based expense (called a premium).

The stock cost recorded in the agreement is known as the "strike cost. Simultaneously, a put options contract gives the purchaser of the agreement the option to sell the stock at a strike cost by a predefined date. In the two cases, if the purchaser of the options contract doesn't act by the assigned date, the choice lapses.

For instance, in a straightforward call options contract, a merchant may expect Company XYZ's stock cost to go up to $90 in the following month. The merchant sees that he can purchase an options agreement of Company XYZ at $4.50 with a strike cost of $75 per share. The dealer must compensation the expense of the alternative ($4.50 X 100 offers = $450). The stock value starts to ascend true to form and settles at $100. Before the expiry date on the options contract, the merchant executes the call alternative and purchases the 100 portions of Company XYZ at $75, the strike cost on his options contract. He pays $7,500 for the stock. The broker would be able to then sell his new stock available for $10,000, making a $2,050 benefit ($2,500 short $450 for the options contract).

Does an Option Contract matter?

Options contracts are a significant apparatus that offers merchants the chance to support their stock positions. Options take into account in the utilized situation on a stock, while moderating the danger of the full buy. Likewise, inland, an options agreement may allow a purchaser to make sure about options contracts on various bundles before executing the buy on any single one, guaranteeing that the purchaser will have the option to gather them all before pushing forward.

1.3 Stocks Trading Vs. Options Trading

Regardless of everything, whether you are a dealer or a financial specialist, your goal is to bring in cash. Your auxiliary goal is to do as such with the worthy base degree of hazard.

One of the significant challenges for new options brokers emerges from not seeing how to utilize options to achieve their money related objectives since options exchange uniquely in contrast to stocks.

Everybody realizes that purchasing something now and selling it later at a more significant expense is the way to benefits. However, that isn't adequate for choice brokers since choice costs don't generally carry on true to form, and this information hole could make dealers leave cash on the table or bring about unforeseen misfortunes.

The Mathematical Tool of Greeks

Experienced stockbrokers don't generally purchase stock. At times they know to undercut—planning to benefit when the stock value decays. Such a large number of beginner choice dealers don't think about the idea of selling options (supported to restrict chance), as opposed to getting them.

Options are exceptionally unique speculation apparatuses, and there is definitely more a broker can do than just purchasing and selling singular options. Options have qualities that are not accessible somewhere else in the speculation universe. For instance, there is a lot of scientific apparatuses (the Greeks) that brokers use to quantify chance. On the off chances that you don't get a handle on exactly how significant that is, consider this:

On the off chance that you can quantify chance (i.e., most extreme increase or misfortune) for a given position, you can likewise limit it. Interpretation: Traders can maintain a strategic distance from awful shocks by realizing how much cash can be lost when the direst outcome imaginable happens.

So also, brokers must know the possible prize for any situation to decide if looking for a potential prize merits the necessary hazard.

For instance, a couple of components that options dealers use to check hazard/reward potential.

Holding a Position for a Specific Time

In contrast to stock, all options lose an incentive over the long haul. The Greek letter "Theta" is utilized to depict how the section of one day influences the estimation of choice.

The Delta

Delta quantifies how a value change, either sequential, for hidden stock or record influences the cost of a choice.

Continuous Price Change

As a stock keeps on moving one way, the rate at which benefits or misfortunes gather changes. That is another method of saying that the choice Delta isn't steady, however, changes. The Greek Gamma portrays the rate at which Delta changes.

It is totally different for stock (regardless of the stock value, the estimation of one portion of stock consistently changes by $1 when the stock value changes by $1), and the idea is something with which another options dealer must be agreeable.

A Changing Volatility Environment

When exchanging stock, a progressively unstable market converts into bigger everyday value changes for stocks. In the options world, changing unpredictability assumes a huge job in evaluating the options. Vega quantifies how much the cost of an alternative change when evaluated instability changes.

Hedging with Spreads

Options are regularly utilized in mix with different options (i.e., get one and sell another). That may sound confounding, yet the overall thought is straightforward: When you have a desire for the hidden resource conduct, for example,

- Bullish
- Bearish
- Neutral (expecting a range-bound market)
- Becoming substantially more, or significantly less, unstable

You can develop places that gain cash when your desires work out as expected. The quantity of potential blends is enormous, and you can discover data on an assortment of options systems that utilization spreads. Spreads have constrained hazards and restricted prizes. Nonetheless, in return for tolerating constrained benefits, spread exchanging accompanies its prizes, for example, an improved likelihood of winning cash. To some degree, traditionalist financial specialist has a major preferred position when ready to possess places that accompany an OK likely benefit—and a high likelihood of winning that benefit. Stock merchants have nothing like choice spreads.

Options exchanging isn't stock exchanging. For the informed alternative broker, that is something worth being thankful for on the grounds that choice systems can be intended to benefit from a wide assortment of securities exchange results. What's more, that can be practiced with constrained hazards.

The Balance doesn't give duty, speculation, or money related administrations and counsel. The data is introduced without thought of the speculation destinations, hazard resistance, or monetary conditions of a particular financial specialist and probably won't be appropriate for all speculators. Past execution isn't demonstrative of future outcomes. Contributing includes hazards, including the conceivable loss of head.

1.4 The Options Jargons

So, turning out to be familiar requires learning some key terms. Here are the basics for starting financial specialists to exchange options.

Strike Price

For one to know whether a stock can be worked out, the strike cost would need to be gauged. There is a value that it should have when a choice gets to the expiry date. This cost ought to be lower or higher than the stock cost, and the strike cost of a basic resource is the thing that we allude to like that. In the event that you expect, as a financial specialist, that the estimation of the stock will rise, you can purchase a call alternative at a value set for the strike. With regards to putting options, the expense of a call will be the cost at which the alternative holder will exchange an advantage when the agreement terminates. The strike cost, as well, perhaps called the activity cost. It is a really critical factor to consider when choosing the estimation of the alternative. The strike cost can change, as indicated by when the options are executed. As a financial specialist, monitoring the strike cost is something to be thankful for as it assists with distinguishing the proficiency of speculation.

Styles

There are two basic models of styles. Those are styles of European and American options. On the off chances or opportunities that you wish to exchange options, it is fitting to outfit yourself with information on the various sorts. You will perceive those that work for you when you assess the models and those that don't. Once in a while, you'll see that particular models are less difficult to comprehend and oversee than others. You may select to take part in the one that is simple for you and quit taking part in a difficult situation understanding.

The American-style choice permits one to exchange any period between the hour of procurement and the hour of expiry of an agreement. Due to its benefit, most dealers take part in this style. This expects one to play out the exchange at any period during which an agreement is viewed as authentic. Contrasted and the American style, the European style choice isn't broadly utilized. A broker can just exercise his/her options during the lapse date in the European choice organization. On the off chances that you aren't an option exchanging master, I would encourage you not to utilize the European kind.

Date of Termination

A termination date alludes to the time after which an agreement is viewed as void. The period between the time they were bought and the expiry date shows a choice's legitimacy. As a seller, during this time range, you should utilize the agreements for your potential benefit. You can trade as much as possible, and get exceptional yields over the purchasing time frame and expiry period. Figure out how to utilize the time accessibly. On the off chances that you are not cautious, the privilege can lapse before you are allowed a chance to practice it.

We will have starters who have faith in this angle and wind up losing gradually. Taking part in the financial exchange would permit you to be mindful. Neglecting to take a gander at the expiry date will prompt your stocks to be esteemed useless without getting an opportunity to put resources into them. The inventories are practiced before the expiry time frame in certain strange cases.

Contracts

Agreements apply to the number of offers that individual intends to buy. One hundred offers in a basic resource compare to an agreement. Agreements help in choosing the estimation of the stock. Agreements will, in general, be significant until the date of expiry. An agreement might be considered invalid after the expiry date. Realizing this will assist you in finding the correct opportunity to pound out an arrangement. For a situation where a broker is purchasing ten options, the individual in question gets 10 $350 calls. In the event that stock qualities go over $350, the seller gets a chance to buy or sell 1000 portions of their stock at $350, at the expiry rate. This happens to pay little mind to the stock cost at that specific time. On an occasion that the stock is underneath $350, the choice terminates uselessly. As a speculator, that will bring about an all-out misfortune. You'll lose the entire sum you used to purchase options, and it is extremely unlikely you can get it back. In case you're trying to put resources into exchanging options, it's fundamental to get mindful of the agreements and how you can practice them for a fruitful exchanging result.

Premium

The premium is true to the cash you used to buy options. You will get the reward by increasing the cost of a call and the number of agreements by 100. The '100' mirrors the number of offers per bargain.

At the point when you choose to take part in stocks, you will run over different terms. We have numerous individuals putting intensely in stocks since they couldn't comprehend the various terms utilized. Not that ought to be the situation. You should set aside some effort to experience the words and completely consider what they mean.

The right, however, not the Commitment

What strikes a chord when perusing this announcement? All things considered, when we talk or have rights, we mean you have the opportunity to purchase such an item. At this point, when we talk about obligation, we apply to the way that one has no legitimate position to play out an obligation. Options don't allow dealers a legitimate option to lead an assignment. This implies the opportunity of exchange exists, yet it isn't lawfully authorized.

Selling or Buying

You are given the options to purchase or trade an alternative as a dealer. There are two kinds of stock from which one can pick. We have the chance to position and the alternative to call. Both recognize, and each has its upsides and downsides.

Setting Explicit Price

There is a particular value set for practicing the right. The cost will shift, as indicated by the kind of item. Some investment opportunities will, in general, be more costly than others. There is an assortment of elements influencing the options rates. At the point when you keep on perusing this book, these angles will come through to you. Realizing them can permit you to comprehend when to lead an exchange, and when not to make an exchange, contingent upon the effect of the components; an exchange can create a high salary or result in misfortune.

Expiry of the Agreement

The expiry date is the point at which an agreement is viewed as useless. Investment opportunities are dated to expiry. The year is set to choose the estimation of choice. Correspondence will be esteemed to be current whenever before the expiry date. This guarantees it tends to be utilized at any phase before the expiry date to deliver incomes. At the point when the expiry date is reached, a merchant has no capacity to practice the right. That is on the grounds that the agreement is viewed as useless. As a financial specialist, it's indispensable to guarantee your venture is reliably inside its legitimacy range.

1.5 Calculating the Margin in Options Trading

Exchanging options are now entangled enough, so you are acquainting a totally different measurement with it when you begin seeing influence exchanging with options. In any case, on the off chances or opportunities that you have a decent comprehension of how edge options work, you ought to have the option to execute techniques that have a factual advantage, for example, credit spreads and calls and puts available to be purchased.

Options are lapsing resources, and on the off chance that you can put on strategies that exploit that, much as the experts and significant organizations do, at that point, you'll arrange the cards in support of yourself.

Edge exchanging with stocks shifts fundamentally from edge exchanging with shares, so how about we investigate what edge is and how it works.

Edge exchanging is the point at which the intermediary acquires cash to situate a deal.

It's similar to a credit provided that you keep the spot for the time being; at that point, you typically need to pay enthusiasm on that advance entirety, yet each merchant is unique, so ensure you talk with them before utilizing an offer.

Edge accounts require a base introductory $2,000 speculation, and you should be pre-endorsed before they open a record for you. This is a quick procedure, and in one day, most merchants will have it finished.

For the edge accounts, there are a couple of things you have to think about. The underlying edge is unique. That is the thing that you'll need to store when you make a request, and it's for the most part around half for stocks, yet it likewise relies upon the dealer. This implies you would have $20,000 in buying power for inventories on the off chance that you have $10,000 in your record.

The following word you'll need to get familiar with is the support edge. This is a significant one, as it is the base parity that you need to keep up before an edge call is given.

An edge call is a point at which you're asked by a representative to store more assets into your record or offer different protections to settle part or the entirety of your advance. At the point when you don't do it when an edge call is made, it will be taken care of by the merchant.

Selling exposed calls or puts is the least secure choice you can exchange, and that is the reason it needs endorsement at the most elevated level. At the point when you sell a stripped call, you are essentially at unending danger, on the grounds that the stock will conceivably go up uncertainly.

Credit spreads, while restricting your hazard, are an incredible method to get cash. These are impressively simpler to figure than bare calls or puts.

Remember that intermediary programming ought to compute this for you naturally so you won't need to do all the figuring; however, it's a smart thought to have a comprehension of how it functions before you hop into it.

Selling options is an extraordinary method to trade options with a benefit, however on the off chance that you don't have the foggiest idea how edge works with them, you may be at serious money related hazard. To utilize these methodologies, you will require an edge account and be affirmed for the degree of the vital alternative.

Chapter 2: Types, Styles, Pros, and Cons of Options Trading

2.1 Types and Styles of Options

There are a few kinds of options that are generally exchanged. These options can be classified into different structures as for the highlights they have. The brad feeling of options has two significant sorts of options. The two options are known as puts and call options. A call alternative can give a purchaser the option to buy a monetary instrument. Then again, options hand an individual the option to sell the benefit. A reasonable qualification is utilized to arrange the alternative, which is' they may be European style or American style. The thought you can wind up having is that the order is done based on geological area, which isn't the situation. The real truth is that the grouping is done in light of where the agreement can be worked out.

The order of the choice procedure goes a step further to utilize the strategy utilized in trading to group them. Different techniques used to recognize the current kinds of options incorporate the necessary security they identify with and the lapse cycle that they contain. This expands singular discoveries to a few types of options that exist over the globe. These options can be all around clarified for a person to comprehend the idea of exchange options. They incorporate;

- **Calls Options**

These options are portrayed by giving an individual the option to buy the concurred resource on a future date. The benefits being purchased will, in general, have a previously settled upon cost.

Certain circumstances can make an individual approach an interest. The most widely recognized situation is when one hypothesizes that the benefit will improve in its Value over a specific timeframe. A trait of calls is that they have an expiry date, which relies on the agreement an individual has entered into. The advantage of being focused on can be purchased before the termination date.

- **Puts Options**

Puts are consistently the specific inverse of calls sort of options. A person who claims the put choice has the privilege gave to him of selling the necessary resources. The way toward offering will, in general, have a concurred value that has been resolved for the future demonstration. This situation occurs during fascinating stages in the money related markets. An individual will probably fall under put activity when the person in question has estimated the estimation of the resources for fall. Notwithstanding being something contrary to the call, there are similitudes among calls and puts. A comparable significant event is that they are both restricted to the time set. In this manner, puts have a termination date on the agreement one has entered.

- **American Style Options**

The American style has nothing identified with purchasing and selling of agreements when it limits options. It concentrates its focal points on the standing that are expressed in the authoritative terms in an understanding. Essential information now is that options accompany a termination date in their agreements, which gives a dealer in the budgetary markets the privilege of either purchasing or selling a fundamental resource. In the American style choice, an individual has the right to practice their agreement before the lapse in the contract. The expressed adaptability will, in general, a preferred position to a broker utilizing American style options.

- **European Style Options**

People who have managed this kind of option are not given similar adaptability experienced by individuals who are utilizing American style contracts. The course of events in this sort of choice is exacting. An individual using European style contracts should just exchange their essential resources on the date of lapse and not previously or after.

- **Trade Traded Options**

It is likewise regularly known as recorded options over the globe to a few money-related market members. It tends to be named as one of the most widely recognized sorts of options known to individuals. There are a few choice agreements that are recorded in the on open trading trades. These are the sorts of options that are alluded to as trade exchange options. They can have the option to be purchased or sold by anybody with the guide of unobtrusive representatives.

- **Over the Counter Options**

This sort of exchange options is just exchanged over the counter markets. These ordinary qualities that compound over the counter exchange options make them not effectively open to the total of the general population. The terms of agreements in these types of exchange options will, in general, be confounded contrasted with different kinds of exchange options.

- **Representative Stock Option**

This type of investment opportunity is known to be introduced to workers. A representative of a specific organization offering alternative can be conceded this agreement by the organization the person is working for.

Their overall use is to encourage compensation to workers. It proceeds to go about as rewards or motivating forces workers of a particular organization are given. It has a few focal points since it pulls in individuals to work for associations that offer such.

- **Money Settled Options**

These sorts of agreements don't describe themselves with the physical exchange of the exchanged resources. What is happens in money settled choice can be identified with the name it has. Benefits made in this sort of alternative are paid in real money structures to the triumphant party. There are sure reasons that happen to this kind of alternative trading. It goes to the event when the benefit being moved is costly or entangled to be transferred to the next gathering.

- **Kinds of Options Based on Expiration**

Agreements have the chance of being characterized by their lapse dates. This identifies with specific marvels that a merchant should have the option to sell as for the set date in an agreement. The contacts concurred that options trading would, in general, vary with the cycles they have. They incorporate;

- **Regular Options**

They depend on the periods the exchange is settled upon and recorded in the agreements. One is probably going to have four termination months to pick in a money related year.

- **Weekly Options**

They were presented in the year 2005 and are otherwise called weeklies. They have the same standards from regular options thought they had diminished timings in them. Weeklies will, in general, be utilized in restricted monetary instruments.

- **Quarterly Options**

They recorded in the trade markets with their termination dates being comparative or close to budgetary quarters. A few people term them as weeklies, and they terminate on the most recent day of lapse.

Sorts of Options by the Underlying Security

An investment opportunity is overall, that has been the center when individuals will, in general discussion about exchange options. This is where the vital resources of going with are openly recorded can be utilized as a monetary instrument. It is regular information on individuals who have put resources into this type of exchange. There are a few sorts of options that are associated with this case, and they incorporate;

- **Stock Options**

An organization that is freely recorded has its offers is, they structure vital resources that are being exchanged in this agreement.

- **Index Options**

They will, in general, have a nearby similitude to the investment opportunities. In any case, there is a distinction that portrays the obscured line. The split comes when the primary type of security being exchanged isn't stocks; rather. They are an organization's files.

- **Currency Options**

This agreement has an away from different types of choice. It is because it gives a dealer the option to either sell or purchase money. The exchange is made at concurred terms of the agreement.

- **Future Options**

The future agreement is the essential resource utilized in this type of option trading. A next Options can give a dealer an option to take an interest in a future agreement.

- **Commodity Option**

The advantage which is underlined in this sort of alternative trading will, in general, be a physical item.

- **Basket Option**

It is a sort of alternative trading that has a few monetary instruments as the necessary resources.

- **Extraordinary Options**

It is a term that is utilized to portray those options gets that have been tweaked by options dealers. The subsequent impact of this customization makes the agreements to be increasingly unpredictable. They are named as Non-Standardized options at times. They are other colorful agreements that are just found in the OTC markets. In any matter, there is a portion of these options gets that have begun being acclaimed in the current budgetary markets. These options include:

- **Barrier Options**

A compensation out is continuously given to a holder of this type of agreement until the minutes the cost expressed in this agreement comes to.

- **Binary Options**

The proprietor of the essential budgetary resources is given a fixed measure of cash in the occasion the agreement terminates.

- **Choose Options**

These type of exchange options permits a money related dealer to pick whether to call or put whenever.

- **Compound Options**

A type of trading choice in which the fundamental budgetary resource is another choice.

2.2 The Pricing Mechanism

A few dealers have picked up the certainty to bring in cash in the securities exchange by discovering a couple of fruitful stocks that will before long make a considerable jump. Be that as it may, if you don't have the foggiest idea of how to utilize the development, you might be left in the residue. In the fact that it seems like you, maybe it's an ideal opportunity to begin using options.

This bit will examine the contemplations that should be weighed to exploit stock variances if you mean to exchange options.

As we told, Options are subsidiaries contracts which offer the holder the right, however not the commitment, to purchase (on account of a call) or to sell (on account of a put) a hidden resource or security at a foreordained cost (called the strike cost) before the agreement lapses. The correct accompanies a value, which is known as the choice premium. Seeing how to gauge the premium is fundamental for trading options and, at last, relies upon the likelihood that the option to purchase or sell winds up being worthwhile at Expiry.

Before entering the trading options world, financial specialists ought to have a decent comprehension of the elements which decide the estimation of an alternative. Those incorporate the current stock value, the intrinsic worth, opportunity to relax esteem, expansion, loan costs, and money profits paid. There are likewise strategies for estimating models that utilization these standards to survey the honest evaluation of a benefit.

Of such, the best perceived is the Black-Scholes model.

From numerous points of view, options are generally similar to some other venture — you have to comprehend what characterizes their cost to utilize them adequately. Different models, including the binomial model and the trinomial model, are likewise generally used.

We should proceed with the key drivers of a choice's Value: flow stock cost, inherent worth, expiry period or period worth, and instability. The original stock cost is quite direct. The progression of the stock cost up or down has a comparative, if not equivalent, the impact on the choice's Value. In case the cost of stock forms, the more likely it is that a call elective's cost will rise, and a put decision's cost will fall. If the stock value falls, the opposite is destined to occur at the expense of the calls and puts.

The Black-Scholes Formula:

The Black Scholes model is presumably the most popular evaluating approach for options. The plan of the model is gotten by increasing the stock cost by the typical total standard circulation capacity of likelihood. The NPV of the strike cost is duplicated by the run of the mill's total usual appropriation and afterward deducted from the subsequent measurement of the recent estimation.

Entangling and overwhelming can be the science engaged with the differential condition that makes up the Black-Scholes recipe. Luckily, you don't need to learn or even comprehend the Math of your methods to utilize Black-Scholes displaying. Options dealers and speculators approach a scope of online options adding machines. A significant number of the present trading stages have thorough instruments for assessing options, including markers and spreadsheets that lead computations and execution estimating options.

Beneath, we'll jump somewhat more profoundly into options cost to clarify what makes up the inborn versus extraneous (time), which means, which is slightly more straightforward.

Characteristic Value:

Characteristic Value is the worth that any given a choice would have whenever practiced today. The inherent quality is the expense by which a choice's strike cost is gainful, or in-the-cash, contrasted with the market cost of the stock. When the choice's strike cost isn't serious compared with the stock value, it is expected that the decision is out of the cash, which implies unfruitful. On the off chance that the hit cost slams into the market cost of the stock, it is expected that the alternative is at-the-cash, practice or not, the choice does not affect the financial specialist.

Albeit intrinsic worth includes the connection between the cost of the strike and the market stock value, it doesn't make up for how much (or how brief period) stays before the Expiry of choice — called Expiry. The measure of time left on alternative effects a choice's premium or worth, which you'll investigate in the following area. Likewise, the intrinsic worth is the part of the cost of a decision that has not been lost or influenced given the progression of time.

The characteristic estimation of some random alternative mirrors the fruitful money related advantage of practicing that choice right away.

Time Value and Time Decay:

Since options contracts have a limited period before they lapse, the rest of the measure of time has a relating financial worth — called Time Value. It is legitimately connected to the time an alternative has at showcase cost before it lapses, just as the vulnerability, or varieties.

The more drawn out an alternative has the opportunity to terminate, the higher the probability that it winds up in cash.

One choice's time parcel rots exponentially. The real derivation of an alternative's time esteem is a genuinely unpredictable condition. A replacement will, by and massive lose 33% of its incentive in the central portion of its life and 66% in the other 50% of its life. This is a basic idea for speculators in protections because the closer the alternative terminates, the more a move in the hidden security is expected to affect the choice's cost.

The time esteem is left of the premium after estimating the intensity in the market between the cost of the strike and the price of the stock. Therefore, the time esteem is alluded to as the Extrinsic Value of choice, since time esteem is the total by which a choice's cost surpasses the inherent worth.

Time esteem is the hazard premium required by the alternative dealer to concede the choice purchaser the option to sell or purchase the stock up to the date the choice terminates. It resembles a discretionary protection premium; the higher the hazard, the higher the expense of buying it.

Instability:

Instability alludes to vacillations in the market cost of the hidden resource comparable to the options advertise. The time estimation of choice likewise relies vigorously upon the Volatility the market anticipates that the stock should show until Expiry.

Regularly, high unpredictability stocks are bound to be gainful or in-the-cash by expiry options. Accordingly, the time esteem — as a bit of the top-notch alternative — is generally higher to relieve the expanded likelihood that the stock cost will transcend the strike cost and lapse in-the-cash. The time estimation of choice will be moderately low for stocks that aren't relied upon to move a lot.

One measurement used to compute unpredictable inventories is called Beta.

Beta tests a stock's unpredictability as contrasted and the general market. Unstable stocks will generally have high betas, mainly on account of stock value unpredictability before the choice terminates. Top beta stocks, despite everything, bear a higher hazard than low beta stocks, in any case. Unpredictability can be known as a double-edged blade, which permits the potential for noteworthy returns for financial specialists, yet instability can likewise prompt significant misfortunes.

The instability impact is frequently emotional and difficult to gauge. Luckily, a few adding machines are accessible to help measure instability. To make this considerably additionally intriguing, there are a few sorts of unpredictability, with the most remarkable being suggested and verifiable. Previously, when financial specialists see vulnerability, it's either called chronicled unpredictability.

Chronicled Volatility (HV) lets you evaluate the conceivable degree of the underlying stock's future developments. Factually, 66% of all stock value occasions ought to happen inside give or take one standard deviation of the move of the capital over a given period. Chronicled instability keeps on thinking back to perceive how dangerous the market was. It permits options for financial specialists to evaluate which exercise cost is generally suitable for picking a specific system.

Suggested Volatility is the thing that current market costs mean and is utilized for hypothetical models. It helps set the current price for an accessible other option and permits players to decide the estimation of an arrangement. Inferred unpredictability tests what options merchants intend to become later on. Inferred unpredictability is a proportion of the market's modern slant. This notion will be reflected in the Value of the option, which will assist dealers in deciding the alternative's future worth and liquidity dependent on current choice costs.

The pace at which the cost of stock changes, called instability, additionally influences the likelihood that an alternative will terminate in the capital. Suggested instability, likewise alluded to as Vega will blow up the exceptional choice if the brokers are anticipating unpredictability.

Suggested instability is typically a proportion of the market's impression of the likelihood that stock cost will increment in esteem. High unpredictability improves a stock's probability of going past the strike cost, so options brokers may request a higher sum for the options they offer.

That is the reason notable occasions, for example, income is in every case, less worthwhile than at first expected for alternative purchasers. Even though there could be a massive change in stock, alternative costs are ordinarily sensibly high before these occasions, which diminishes the potential benefits.

In the examination, when a stock cost is small, the cost of options keeps on declining, making them sensibly modest to buy. Until instability increments once more, nonetheless, the choice stays modest and practically rules out benefit.

The worth or premium of an alternative is determined by the qualities natural and extraneous. The moneyness of choice is inherent worth, while the external Value has more parts. Consider the variables in play when booking trading options, and give passage and leave plan.

2.3 The Pros of options trading

We've seen that trading options are a movement that has its upsides and its drawbacks. In this portion, we will have a look at the top reasons you need to exchange options. Remember that you can customize your portfolio and speculation technique, so it's not essential to go "all in" with regard to trading options. You can have options trading as one piece of a different venture procedure. Numerous individuals use options to cover dangers in various sections of their general portfolio.

Trading Options gives a venture opportunity restricted capital

Take a circumstance where we started with a model demonstrating that for $250, you could control 100 portions of stock that would cost somebody $3,900 to purchase inside and out. At that point, we developed that and saw what sort of potential outcomes existed when contributing more significant sums. Nonetheless, if you are merely beginning with adding, it's not essential to purchase more than each options contract in turn. You can provide for a moderately modest quantity of cash contingent upon the stock. Trading doesn't need to be drawn closer with a win or bust mindset. You can begin with little ventures and stir your way up by reinvesting your benefits.

You can fence your dangers with file reserves

The vast majority who put resources into stocks will put resources into record assets to have a broadened portfolio. By using options, you can fence your dangers with file reserves. List puts can assist you with alleviating misfortunes if the market encounters a significant downturn. Brilliant financial specialists will use record puts, so the next recession doesn't leave them with colossal troubles.

Benefit off of different misfortunes

Alright, it sounds awful when expressed that way. You can utilize puts to benefit from downturns in stock costs. This is an open door that isn't accessible while doing standard stock trading.

Gather Premiums

As we'll see, there are approaches to benefit from doing as such; however, regardless, you can stash the premiums. This is another approach to acquire cash in a general speculation portfolio that utilizes differing techniques just as various ventures.

Profit by outsized additions

Perhaps the most significant advantage that accompanies trading options has the option to control a lot of stock that could have an immense upside if there is a considerable increment in stock cost by buying countless call options. Being a seer isn't commonly a rewarding pay, yet you can expand your odds of progress via cautiously examining the business sectors and the organizations behind the individual stocks. Search for dynamic regions where new organizations could see a tremendous addition in the stock cost over a brief period. The hazard is that you'll lose your premium on the off chance that the strike cost isn't outperformed, yet on the off chance that it is, at that point, you'll get an opportunity to score enormously. We previously indicated a straightforward model with arrival on 140% speculation, yet it's even conceivable to get an ROI of 500% or much more.

Options are adaptable

At the point when you are working with options, you will find that you get a tremendous amount of adaptability. You can decide to purchase or sell, go with various lapse dates, pick from an assortment of techniques and resources, and even have authority over your strike cost.

There are also ways that you will have the option to benefit if the market goes down. Some of the time, this adaptability is going to make working in options increasingly entangled. Yet, if you realize what you are doing, this kind of versatility will assist you with profiting, paying little mind to how the market is getting along.

Addition influence

Another advantage you will have the option to get when you choose to work with the possibilities advertise is influence. To keep things straightforward, control is a significant favorable position to the dealer. When you gain control, you give yourself more options since you can place more cash into the market without expecting to have more startup funding to get you out. This can be risky because it makes you lose more cash than you have in the first place, yet if you are cautious and perused the market right, it will get you gain a ton more cash-flow even with lower startup costs.

2.4 The cons of options trading

Lower Liquidity

Various individual venture openings don't have a great deal of volume in any way, shape, or form. The method that each option able stock will have options exchanging at different strike expenses and terminations suggests that the particular decision you are exchanging will be lacking volume aside from on the off chance that it is one of the most notable stocks or stock records. This more inferior liquidity won't make any difference a lot to a little dealer that is trading only ten agreements, however.

Higher Spreads

Options will, in general, have higher ranges on account of the absence of liquidity.

This implies it will cost you more in roundabout costs while doing an alternative exchange since you will be surrendering the spread when you exchange.

Higher Commissions

Options exchanges will cost you more in commission per dollar contributed. These commissions might be significantly higher for spreads where you need to pay commissions for the two sides of the range.

Confused

Options are confused about tenderfoots. Most amateurs, and even some propelled financial specialists, thought they comprehended them when they don't.

Decay of Time

When you are purchasing options, you lose the time estimation of the options while holding them. There are no individual cases to this standard.

Less Data

Options can be an agony when it is more diligently to get cites or other standard expository data like the inferred unpredictability.

Options not Accessible for all Stocks

Even though options are convenient on a decent number of shares, this, despite everything, limits the number of conceivable outcomes available to you.

Chapter 3: Options Trading and Risk Management

Since we recognize what drives choice costs, we should make it increasingly quantifiable. This is finished utilizing the alleged "Greeks," five boundaries indicated by Greek images (or letters), which measure how a choice's cost will change. You don't have to know accurately how they work, exactly what they state. You can admire them at some random chance to get their qualities. We start by taking a gander at characteristic worth, specifically how the choice value changes or fluctuates with the cost of the hidden stock.

You will see five Greek letters (generally spoke to by their English spelled names) Delta, Theta, Gamma, Vega, and Rho in the event that you take a gander at the information for any choice.

3.1 Delta (D)

The first is Delta (Δ), which gives you how the cost of an alternative change with the basic stock cost.

We expressed before that there is no 1-1 move-in cost concerning the stock at the cost of a choice. By taking a gander at Delta, you will see exactly how it would change.

From the start, we should discover the options to call. Thus, if Delta is 0.46, this implies if the basic stock cost goes up by $1, the alternative cost will go up by $0.46. In the event that Delta is 0.74, at that point, the alternative cost would increment by $0.74 if the fundamental stock cost expanded by $1.

Put options have a negative delta, which just implies that a put alternative has a converse connection to the basic stock cost.

That is, if the basic stock's value falls, the estimation of a put alternative ascents, and if the fundamental stock's cost goes up, the estimation of the put choice falls.

Along these lines, if Delta were - 0.26, and the basic stock cost goes up by $1, the put alternative's worth would decrease by 26 pennies. Then again, in the event that the fundamental stock cost had fallen by $1, at that point, the put alternative cost would go up by $0.26.

Delta is dynamic, and when any huge boundary changes in the value options, the sum will consistently change. Discover an alternative on a stock valued at $102 with a $100 strike cost, with a lapse of 14 days to offer. The call alternative cost is $2.48 for this situation, and Delta is 0.75 all things considered. Put alternative rates are $0.47 and put choice differential is - 0.25. What's more, on the off chances that the stock value ascends by $1, at that point, we anticipate that the call choice should ascend to $2.48 + $0.75 = $3.23. The put alternative's cost would tumble to $0.47-$ 0.25=$0.22.

That is just about what's happening. However, truth be told, the relationship isn't entirely dependable in light of the fact that different elements influence the cost of the options. The truth would have been that the call alternative ascents to $3.84, and the put choice abatements to $0.27 in cost.

We have said it is mind-boggling, and what happens when the offer cost increments by $1, is additionally the Delta esteems for the two options. Presently consider Delta for the call is 0.84, and - 0.16 for put.

That reveals to us something significant, to be specific that the higher the Delta, the more the stock is in cash.

Since the more cash you are in, at that point, the Delta is higher, which implies that a $1 change in the cost of the fundamental stock will pick up (or be hurt by) in the cash options.

Something else that happens is that the closer you get to expiration, the higher Delta goes when the alternative is held. For our case of a $100 share value alternative, if the fundamental stock value remains at $103, moving from expiry to 7 days, Delta jumps for the call to 0.92. Moving to the expiry of 3 days, the Delta is 0.98. In this way, in the event that you anticipate that a stock cost should change a great deal in the following not many days, it could be beneficial speculation to get a choice that will terminate without further ado before the move occurs. Search for occasions that may affect the cost, for example, a call to profit or a declaration of a buy.

Note that the cash options have a delta of around 0.50, and when you draw near to development, the Delta for a call will be actually 0.50, and for a put, it will be - 0.5, if the cash alternative is in. It tends to be testing really to purchase at the cash options, so you'll most likely need to agree to something comparable.

On the off chance that an alternative is out of the range, you get the littler delta drawing nearer to the lapse date. In all actuality, it can turn out to be vanishingly little a couple of days from the expiry delta. A choice out of the cash offer at a $100 strike cost, a $97 share cost with three days to lapse, would have a 0.02 delta.

The Delta should summarize the distinction to 100 for a similar put choice (however note it's communicated as a negative worth). For this situation, a put alternative with similar conditions, so a $100 strike cost – if the basic cost is $97, would have a delta of - 0.98. The put would be worth $3.00 in that circumstance, and if the hidden offer cost tumbled to $96, the put cost would increment to $4. You will, at that point, see the Delta ascend to - 1.00 for putting and reduction to 0.00 for calling.

In the event that the stock went the other way, the cost expanded by $1; at that point, the Delta for the put would drop to - 0.92, and the put cost would drop to $2.04.

The main concern is Delta should give you a reasonable estimation of how much the choice cost should change if the fundamental stock cost increments by $1. In the events that this is a possibility for calling, the relationship is immediate, and the Delta is communicated as a positive number. For put options, on the grounds that the connection is the inverse, the Delta is a negative number. Also, note that in the events that you take the outright delta esteem for the put alternative and apply it to the delta esteem for a considered choice that has a similar strike worth and termination date, it will indicate 1.0.

3.2 Gamma (G)

Gamma (G) is a subordinate of the Delta. In other words, and it gives you how the Delta changes itself. This is critical as we found the Delta was dynamic. Beginning dealers don't have to dive too profoundly into this, however, so you can test Gamma to perceive the amount Delta can change if the cost of the fundamental offers increments by $1. For the two puts and calls, Gamma has a similar worth. What's more, if Gamma were 0.22 and Delta was 0.24 for a Call Option, and - 0.76 for a Put Option of a similar strike and lapse date, we would expect a $1 ascend in share cost would trigger a Delta raise for the call choice to 0.46, and the PUT choice delta will acclimate to - 0.54. This is about what will occur, however, recall whether the alternative was to move the Delta esteems to 0.5 and - 0.5, separately, at the cash.

3.3 Theta (Q)

Theta (Q) is an exceptionally critical boundary among the Greeks while examining options. Theta gives you insights concerning is the choice's time rot. Theta is communicated as a negative number, speaking to the way that time rot over the long haul causes a decrease in the cost of options. We should take in a couple of models.

Assume we have a call and put options at a $100 hit cost with three days to lapse. The call cost is $1.20, and the put cost is $0.20 if the basic stock cost is $101. For this situation, for both the call and the put theta is - 0.073. That discloses to us that if nothing else changes, every choice's cost will go down $0.073. The call alternative is $1.20, and the put is $0.20. Moving to 2 days before lapse and leaving all else the equivalent, we see the call choice-value tumbling to $1.12, and the put alternative value tumbling to $0.12, so it moved correctly to what exactly was arranged. The following day theta has ascended to - 0.079, mirroring the way that time rot happens faster, the closer you get to the alternative's expiry date.

Twenty days to the termination theta, with everything else unaltered, is about half as high, at - 0.035.

This speaks to one of the fundamental facts of options; that is, time rot happens exponentially, with time rot happening quicker the closer you get to the termination.

One of the components that can cause answers for seem confounding is the association of these factors. In this way, envision the stock value shot up to $108 at 20 days to expiry. All things considered, Theta is down to - 0.005. Along these lines, this is the only 1/seventh of the past worth. It diminishes in any event, for the choice of putting.

In like manner, Theta is relative to the offer cost. Also, if the offer cost is higher, the Theta is littler. Consider a stock that has a $975 share cost, and a $1,000 strike cost. All things considered, Theta is - 0.282 for the alternative call, and - 0.274 for the choice put. That implies the estimation of the call alternative (which for this situation is $5.15) will drop by around $0.28 if a day passes, and nothing else changes, and the estimation of the put choice will drop by about $0.27.

The key exercise here is equivalent to it was previously, that with regards to valuing options, time rot is a significant major one. Test the Greek Theta for a sign of whether the choice's cost would diminish by the following day if every single other thing is considered equivalent.

3.4 Vega (n)

The next Greek we'll encounter is Vega (n), which tells us the relation between the option price and the volatility implied. What Vega tells you is how sensible the option is to alter the volatility meant. Generally speaking, an option in money is less sensitive to changes in implied volatility, while an option out of cash is more sensitive to changes in implied volatility. In particular, Vega informs you how much the option price would change if the volatility suggested changes by 1 percent. Remember, options which mean higher volatility are worth more money.

Suppose a stock trades at $500 a share, and the strike price is $490 with ten days left to expire and an associated 23.5 percent volatility. Vega is 0.285. A call would be valued at $13.73, and $3.69 will be evaluated for the put with the same parameters. If the volatility implied was increased to 24.5 percent, the call would be priced at $14.02, and the put would be $3.98. So, in other words, Vega tells you how much the price of the options increases in implied volatility for every point. The closer you get to the date of expiration, the smaller the Vega is getting.

Vega is positive when you are in long positions, and it's negative for short positions.

3.5 Rho (r)

Rho (**r**) is a count of the flexibility of estimating options against a hazard-free loan fee alteration. Since loan costs nowadays don't change by that much or that regularly, rho isn't given a lot of consideration. Rho will be an increasingly noteworthy boundary to focus on in a drastically advancing high-loan fee setting, for example, that which happened in the late 1970s.

Equation of Black-Scholes

The condition of Black-Scholes is a numerical model that clarifies how subordinates resemble options. The choice is actualized as an element of the basic stock cost and time, portfolio instability, and hazard-free loan cost. The condition reveals to us Gamma is a profit by holding a choice. The condition gives us the profits "riskless," where Gamma adjusts the rot of Theta. The Black-Scholes condition requires some sensibly propelled science.

In the event that they are keen on having a superior comprehension of the condition, those with the information and mastery should look into data. It's a halfway differential condition, which can foresee an alternative's future cost. Be that as it may, most alternative dealers couldn't care less about the Black-Scholes condition.

You can basically utilize instruments, for example, spreadsheets or online models that individuals have created to bring the condition energetically for you, and you can play with the different contributions to foresee the conceivable value developments of options in which you are included.

In financial matters, the model has added to a Nobel Laureate. One critical truth is that the model is intended to work with European options that must be utilized at the expiry date and that it doesn't work with American options. Be that as it may, for American options, a few scientific models work well overall.

Chapter 4: Getting Deeper into the Options Pricing

4.1 Moving Averages

The Moving Average is an essential specialized examination technique that smooth out market information by creating a normal value that is consistently refreshed. The normal is assumed control over a given period, for example, ten days, 20 minutes, 30 weeks, or whatever period the merchant picks. There are benefits in your exchanging utilizing a moving normally, just as options on what kind of moving normal to utilize. Moving normal procedures are likewise normal, and can be redone to coordinate both long haul financial specialists and transient dealers whenever outline. A Moving Average (MA) is a usually utilized specialized marker that smoothest showcase designs by sifting through the "clamor" from arbitrary changes for the time being. Moving midpoints can be worked from various perspectives, and for the normal time frame, recruit an alternate number of days. The most that moving normal applications is to characterize pattern bearing and to decide levels of help and opposition. At the point when resource costs cross their moving midpoints, it can give specialized brokers an exchanging signal. Albeit moving midpoints are adequately valuable all alone, they structure the reason for the following specialized markers like the moving normal union uniqueness, as well.

A normal moving assists with chopping a value graph down on the volume of "clamor". To get a basic thought of how the cost is going, take a gander at the bearing of the moving normal. In the event that it's calculated up, the general value goes up, and when calculated down, the absolute value moves down, the cost is as a rule inside a range.

In like manner, a moving normal may fill in as help or opposition. In an upswing, a 100-day or 200-day moving normally will fill in as a help point. This is really on the grounds that the normal fills in as a story (support), so the value ricochets off the level. A moving normal will fill in as obstruction in a downtrend; like a cutoff, the value arrives at the level and afterward goes down once more. In that manner, the cost doesn't generally "regard" the moving normal. The cost will go through it marginally, or stop and opposite until it is reached.

When in doubt, the pattern is up when the cost is over a moving normal. On the off chances that the cost is lesser than a moving normal, at that point, the pattern is down. Moving midpoints may be that as it may, have various lengths, so one MA can demonstrate an upswing while another MA shows a downtrend.

Types of Moving Averages

There are different methods of assessing a moving normally. A basic moving normal of five days called Simple Moving Average (SMA) includes the five latest day by day shutting costs and splits them by five to manufacture another normal every day. Each normal interfaces with the following one, shaping a solitary streamline. It is a straightforward number juggling normal figuring.

$$SMA = \frac{A_1 + A_2 + \cdots + A_n}{n}$$

$A_i = Average\ in\ period/day\ i$

$n = number\ of\ time\ periods/days\ (tipically\ 5\ days)$

The Exponential Moving Average (EMA) is another basic type of moving midpoint. The estimation is increasingly confounded, as all the more weighting is applied to the current qualities.

$EMA_{today} = EMA_{yesterday} \cdot (1 - \alpha) + \alpha \cdot V_{today}$

$\alpha = \dfrac{2}{n + 1}$

$n = number\ of\ days$

On the off chances that you plot a 50-day SMA and an additional 50-day EMA on a similar guide, you will find that as a result of the extra weighting of ongoing value information, the EMA reacts more rapidly to value changes than does the SMA.

The counts are finished by graphing programming and exchanging stages, so no manual Math are required to utilize a moving normally.

A specialized graph demonstrating the exponential moving normal (EMA) and the basic moving normal (SMA) is no superior to one type of MA. For a period, an EMA may work best in stock or monetary market, and an SMA may work better at specific occasions. As far as possible, picked for a moving normal will likewise assume a fundamental job in the manner it is fruitful (paying little heed to type).

Moving Average Length

10, 20, 50, 100, and 200 are moving normal lengths. Contingent upon the time range of the broker, these lengths can be reached out to any diagram time period (one moment, day by day, week by week, and so on.).

The time span or length you decided for a moving normal, likewise called the "look back period," additionally assumes a significant job in how fruitful it is. A MA with a brief timeframe edge can react a lot snappier to cost increments than a MA with a long look back period. The 20-day moving normal tracks the genuine value better than the 100-day moving normally does when expounded in a graph.

The 20-day can be of an expository incentive to a shorter-term broker since it intently coordinates the cost and accordingly shows less "slack" than the drawn-out moving normally. A 100-day MA can be increasingly significant to a merchant in the more drawn out term.

Slack is the time it takes to flag an expected reversal to a moving normal. Note that when the cost is over a moving normal, the pattern is known as an overall rule. In this way, when the value falls underneath that moving normal, a potential inversion fixated on that MA is flagged. A 20-day moving normal can create significantly more "inversion" signals than a moving normal of 100 days.

Any length can be a moving normal: 15, 28, 89, and so forth. Changing the moving normal to give progressively solid signs on verifiable information may help produce better signs later on.

Trading Strategy - Crossover

Hybrids are one of the fundamental techniques for moving midpoints.

The principal sort is a value spike, which is the point at which the cost goes above or under a moving normal to flag a potential pattern move.

Another method is to add two moving midpoints to a line: one longer and one shorter. It is a purchase signal when the momentary MA traverses the more drawn out term MA, as it implies that the pattern is moving upward. This is viewed as a "brilliant cross." Meanwhile, when the momentary MA crosses underneath the more drawn out term MA, it is a selling signal, as it shows a descending pattern. This is known as the "heavenly attendant of death."

4.2 The Momentum

To comprehend the essentialness and helpfulness of force dealers, it is basic to realize what "energy" signifies and its comprehension of exchanging.

Webster's Dictionary depicts momentum as "the force or force acquired through movement or occasion development". These merchants, one of a few unique sorts of stockbrokers, are searching for development in the value, income, or income of stock. The dealers would then regularly take a long or short stock situation with the desire that their energy would move in either an upward or descending bearing. This technique is centered more on transient market vacillations than on essential organization particulars and isn't suggested for beginners.

Henceforth energy brokers trade stocks on high volume that are moving drastically one way. The measure of time a broker keeps his/her situation in exchange relies upon how quickly the stock moves.

Force brokers are essentially a solitary network of individuals. Not at all, like different merchants or investigators are analyzing the budget summaries or outline patterns of business. A "force dealer" is concerned distinctly with stocks in the press. Try not to liken force stock exchanging with the generally watched design exchanging.

Energy isn't really equivalent to the example. There are a ton of stocks with unobtrusive examples, yet they don't change an excessive amount of consistently. In a short casing of time, we have to see a pivotal turning point! In a play of force options, we bring in cash not from diminishing time premium (Theta), or a move in unpredictability (Vega), yet from value development. Energy stock outlines, for the most part, show longer candles, exact developments in the course, and graph holes.

Stocks that move up or down significantly are consistently the casualties of supposition shifts. Financial specialists feel bullish, and afterward, the stock gets overbought or enters a diagram area of specialized obstruction, and auctions.

We have finished up in the wake of seeing a few graphs that the affirming force stocks have a "fan base, (for example, AAPL, TSLA, WYNN) and show enormous value variances. The stock wavers among overbought and oversold. Be that as it may, presently, none of these could be in energy! You, despite everything, need to follow the signs which hit the energy.

To be a decent energy dealer, you must have the psychological solidarity to resist the urge to panic when things go your direction and trust that objectives will be met at this point. Energy exchanging includes a gigantic demonstration of the center, an extraordinary quality of character that makes momentary force exchanging one of the harder types of making a benefit.

Force exchanging is directed as a day exchanging technique, and in this way, time and timing are critical, can happen decently fast.

Successful energy merchants need a one of a kind blend of both basic (occasion-based) and specialized investigation.

Choosing the Momentum Strategies

Here we will quickly make reference to some force exchange techniques to begin seeing how you can make benefit from the choice market in various manners.

- **Short or purchase stock**

The hazard is restricted to the general speculation, despite the fact that brokers seldom pass up a solitary arrangement.

- **Purchase a Call or a Put**

Note the stock trade options can be utilized. We suggest utilizing In-the-Money options with a Delta of at any rate 0.7 (or - 0.7 for a Put) and preferably above 0.9 (or - 0.9 for a Put), on the grounds that these options intently take after stock conduct. Know, the higher the Delta, the more profound it is, and the more costly it is to ITM (in cash). Obviously, the hazard is constrained to the cost of the agreement, which will be a lot less expensive than the stock cost.

The most serious hazard is to purchase OTM (out of the cash) "Puts and Calls," which regularly terminate uselessly. Indeed, even the options that ATM (at the cash) has purchased are normally not a decent technique for in excess of a few days, as time rot begins to evacuate premium.

- **Sell a credit spread**

It is fundamental to situate an OTM credit spread at the assistance and distance from the current cost. The hazard is restricted to the contrast between the strikes short the measure of credit you get.

An ITM credit spread ought to be adequately wide to guarantee that the sold leg (your lucrative leg) has a Delta of in any event 0.9 (or - 0.9 for a Put). Rather than purchasing a Put, a few merchants sell DITM (Deep in the Money) Calls. You would anticipate that the cost should be moving ceaselessly from the bought or sold strike for all credit choice circumstances. The hugest bit of leeway is that you're not doing combating the disintegration of time.

- **Purchase a charge spread**

You decrease your complete expense or hazard by buying one leg and selling another; however, you likewise limit your salary. These are best utilized for transient play, where a little move is envisioned. On the off chances that this is your arrangement, however, why not accepting a call, at that point sell a call later to pull in as much cash as the main call. Your net expense would be zero or better, and your shortfall is zero too.

- **Energy Day Trade**

When in doubt, stocks that open generously lower (from the end of the day preceding) will keep on running down until they have been totally used. The opposite is genuine, as well: stocks that open higher will proceed for quite a while to come. This normality can be traded for benefit. This is much progressively valid for files, for example, the SPY, RUT, or QQQ, as higher volume bolsters these energy patterns over an assortment of stocks. Purchase an ITM alternative utilizing Long Put or Call options and close utilizing stop-limit orders to ensure your advantage. This procedure additionally works for stocks that show a beta of 1.0-1.5.

- **Concerning other Strategies**

They will be treated on day 7; it might be productive to have a long ride or choke; however, note that you are paying twofold for the system, and that cost would need to drop far to make you gainful. A secured call could be worthwhile, yet by setting the short call, the potential advantage will be diminished.

- **Stop strategies that are non-directional**

For example, Iron Condors or short rides. These ought to be evaded in light of the fact that one leg in an energy play could without much of a stretch be crossed.

4.3 Support and Resistance

The standards of help and opposition at the exchanging level are, undoubtedly, two of the highlights of specialized examination most talked about. Dealers utilize those terms as a component of the investigation of outline patterns to allude to value rates on diagrams that seem to go about as impediments, preventing a benefit's cost from being moved a particular way.

From the start, the importance and rule behind these levels appear to be anything but difficult to perceive, yet as you will discover, backing and opposition can come in different manners, and the definition is harder to comprehend than it appears from the start.

Specialized experts use levels of help and protection from characterize value focuses on a graph where the chances favor a split or inversion of a predominant example.

Bolster exists when a downtrend because of the convergence of interest should stop.

Opposition happens when an upswing, because of a flexible focus, is required to delay immediately.

Market brain research assumes a noteworthy job in helping dealers and financial specialists to remember the past and responding to changing conditions to foresee potential market developments.

The pattern lines and moving midpoints can be utilized to characterize territories of help and opposition on diagrams.

The backing is a value point where a downtrend because of an assembly of interest or buying interest might be required to stop. On the off chances that the cost of advantages or protections decays, the interest for the offers rises in this manner shaping the helpline. In the interim, opposition zones rise as costs ascend because of selling esteem.

On the off chance that a zone or "locale" of help or opposition is set up, such value levels will fill in as conceivable section or leave focuses on the grounds that, when a value arrives at a state of help or obstruction, it can do one of two things — skip once again from the degree of help or opposition, or penetrate the degree of cost and move toward its — until it hits the following degree of help or obstruction.

A few exchanges are paced dependent on the desire that zones of help and obstruction won't be disturbed. On the off chances that the measure of help or restriction ends the cost, or it gets through, brokers may "offer" toward the path and rapidly choose if they are right. On the off chances that the cost is going off course, you can close the spot at a little misfortune. In any case, if the value moves the correct way, the change can be considerable.

The Basics

Some accomplished brokers will recount tales about how some value rates seem to debilitate dealers from moving toward any path the cost of a basic resource. For instance, assume Jim held a situation in stock among March and November and anticipated that the estimation of the offers should rise.

Envision Jim seeing the value attempting to get above $39 a few times more than a while, despite the fact that it's verged on getting past that point. In this situation, brokers will call a degree of obstruction around $39 to the value point. As you can see from the diagram, paces of opposition are frequently called a breaking point, since these value limits reflect places where a meeting comes up short on gas.

On the opposite side of the coin, help rates are on. Bolster alludes to the costs on a graph that seem to fill in as a story by forestalling descending pushing of an advantage's cost. The capacity to perceive a help level can likewise associate with a motivation to purchase as this is generally the locale where advertise members discover worth and begin driving up costs once more.

The Trend Lines

This static hindrance is one of the predominant sorts of help/obstruction, yet monetary resource costs normally pattern upwards or downwards, so it's not uncommon to see such value boundaries change after some time. That is the reason pattern definitions and trend lines are pertinent when pondering help and obstruction.

At the point when the market flips around, paces of opposition are built up as the stock value diminishes and starts to move back to the trend line. This is because of benefit taking or close term instability for a given issue or market. The subsequent market activity experiences a "level" impact or a little abatement in the securities exchange, which delivers a transient high.

Numerous brokers would follow through on cautious thoughtfulness regarding the cost of a product when it falls toward the trend line's progressively broad help in light of the fact that, customarily, this has been a domain that has prevented the advantage's cost from falling a lot of lower. For instance, a trend line may give numerous long stretches of help to a benefit.

Additionally, as the market moves downwards, brokers can search for a progression of diminishing pinnacles and look to interface these tops alongside a trend line. At the point when the value comes to the trend line, most merchants will be searching for selling pressure from the benefit and may consider entering a short position since this is a domain that has driven the cost down before.

A characterized degree of help/obstruction, regardless of whether found with a trend line or by some different procedure, is viewed as higher the more occasions the cost has customarily been not able to move past. Most specialized brokers would utilize their characterized degree of help and protection from select vital passage/leave focuses, as these regions regularly speak to the costs generally pertinent to the bearing of a benefit. Most merchants are secure in the basic estimation of the product at these rates, and the volume, as a rule, rises more than normal, making it a lot harder for brokers to keep pushing the cost up or down.

Rounding Numbers

Another regular attribute of help/obstruction is that the cost of a benefit may make some troublesome memories going past a round number, like $50 or $100 an offer. Most fledgling dealers want to purchase or sell resources when the value hits an entire number since they are bound to accept a stock at these rates is sensibly estimated. The greater part of the objective costs or stop orders set by either retail financial specialists or critical venture banks are put at round value rates as opposed to costs like $50.06. Since such a huge number of requests are put at a similar point, these adjusted numbers will, in general, go about as considerable boundaries to the cost. In the event that, for instance, all the clients of a speculation bank put in selling orders at a recommended focus of $55, it would take an extraordinary number of buys to ingest those deals, and in this way, make a degree of opposition.

Moving Averages

Most specialized merchants influence the intensity of different specialized markers to help gauge potential momentary development, for example, moving midpoints, yet these dealers never completely comprehend the limit of such gadgets to characterize backing and opposition rates. A constantly moving line is a moving normal that smooth out past value information while as yet empowering the broker to decide backing and obstruction.

Merchants may utilize moving midpoints in a few different ways, for example, foreseeing developments upward when exchanging lines traverse a focal moving normal or leaving exchanges when costs fall under a moving normal. In the manner the moving normal is utilized, it additionally delivers degrees of "programmed" backing and opposition. Most brokers can analyze in their moving midpoints with various time ranges, so they can locate the one that fits best for this specific crucial.

4.4 Trend Lines

Trend lines are a clear, however successful technique (examining market diagrams) utilized in specialized examination. They serve to light up the overall bearing of the value development of stock.

Trend lines depend on the idea that a stock, or market, is moving in designs (upwards, downwards, and sideways). Costs can be accepted to proceed towards pattern until the pattern is broken.

Patterns can be restricted to three timescales:

- Short Term Trend
- Average Term Trend
- Long Term Trend

There is no set time period (days, weeks, months, and so forth.) that can characterize any of these. It relies upon which time period you are alluding to for diagramming. A day by day stock outline of a half year would have alternate importance for a short, middle of the long road, and long haul design than an everyday diagram of one month.

Maybe the most significant thing is to utilize each of the three-time spans to give you a major in the general image of the activities of the stock. You can likewise utilize every one of the three-time spans to guarantee that you "swim with and not against the occasion" Have you at any point had a go at rowing a sail, or swimming against momentum in the stream? It is extreme! You utilize the entirety of this time and duty, and you are not really going anyplace. Going against the flow isn't a smart activity except if you have a particular reason for that. All things considered, the pattern bearing exchanging "against" is decisively something very similar. It very well done, and you may likewise bring in cash; however, it's smarter to exchange a similar pattern bearing as it will amplify your odds of making a benefit. Continuously take a gander at the short, middle of the road, and long haul patterns to ensure you remain in line with the overall financial exchange heading.

The overall general guideline is that drawing the trend line requires two focuses, and a third point affirms the line's legitimacy. The scores are the value pinnacles or lows.

The trend line is getting increasingly strong as more costs contact the line.

There are three sorts of patterns:

- **Downward Trend (Bearish)**

At the point when costs have dropped, a descending trend line is utilized. By drawing a straight line across value highs, you manufacture a descending trend line. All value movement is beneath the trend line.

Make sure you have the same number of value highs as you can to hit the line, however not all focuses must be on the heading precisely.

The descending pattern is viewed as flawless at insofar as costs stay beneath the trend line. Bearish exchanging techniques and descending trend lines are another extraordinary commendations.

- **Upward Trend (Bullish)**

At the point when costs appear to be rising, an upward trend line is utilized. By drawing a straight line "up and right" overvalue lows, an upward trend line is developed: ensure you have the same number of value lows as you can to arrive at the line, yet not all focuses must be precisely on the line. The upturn is viewed as flawless at insofar as costs remain over the trend line. Bullish exchanging methodologies and upward trend lines supplement each other enormously.

- **Side to Side (Channeling)**

A pattern from side to side is likewise called a channel. It's when stock costs have vacillated between two equal value boundaries. You draw a flat line overvalue highs AND value lows to make the trend lines for a channel. The region between the two lines is known as the trench. Trend lines Prices are limited by lines lit up by two equal value hindrances. The upper edge is, for the most part, alluded to as the degree of opposition, and the lower line is alluded to as the degree of help. Numerous merchants wrongly think a pattern is changing simply because the stock cost is shutting beneath the trend line.

Trend lines are, for the most part, used to screen exchanges and assist you with seeing whether or if the pattern is evolving.

4.5 Candlestick Analysis

Candlestick examination centers on explicit candles to peruse signs about where the market is going. The basic speculation is that the value, as of now, mirrors all known data. Typically, the procedure is joined with help and obstruction. Each flame contains four kinds of valuable data: the high, the low, the open, and the nearby. The net value variance among open and close mirrors a light body while the wicks show inversions that happened inside the flame's time span.

Along these lines, each candle gives a cognizant image of the value activity. The wicks length versus the body length joined with whether a flame is bullish or bearish, can be utilized to break down a sign at the future cost activity. In this examination, standard candles are dojis, turning tops, hammers, inundating candles, pin bars, and inside bars.

To make a candle outline, you need a lot of information containing open, high, low, and close qualities for the period you need to introduce. The empty or filled candle partition is classified "the body." The long flimsy lines above and beneath the body show the high/low range and are known as "shadows." The head of the upper shadow speaks to the high and the low by the lower shadow's base. On the off chance that the stock closes higher than its initial value, an empty candle with the body base speaking to the initial cost and the body top speaking to the end cost is drawn. In the event that the stock closes underneath its initial value, the head of the body is outlined with a filled candle speaking to the initial cost and the base of the body speaking to the end cost.

Candle outlines and bar graphs show similar data, just in an alternate way. Because of the shading coding of the value bars and thicker genuine bodies, candle graphs are progressively visual, which are smarter to feature the distinction between the open and the nearby.

The chart above shows a similar trade exchanged store (ETF) over a similar timeframe. The lower outline utilizes hued bars while the upper diagram utilizes hued candles. A few brokers will, in general, kindness seeing the thickness of the genuine bodies, while others favor bar graphs that moderately look perfect.

Numerous dealers view candle outlines as more outwardly engaging and simpler to decipher contrasted and customary bar diagrams. Every candle outline gives a basic, outwardly engaging image of value activity. A merchant can quickly look at the connection between the open and close, just as the high and low. The open-finished close connection is viewed as imperative data and structures the pith of candles. Empty candles show buying pressure where the end is higher than the open. Filled candles demonstrate selling pressure where the nearby is not exactly open.

4.6 Benefits and Importance of Technical Analysis

The specialized investigation is an exchanging discipline used to evaluate speculations and distinguish exchanging openings by dissecting patterns accumulated from exchanging action, for example, value development and volume.

In contrast to the major examination, which looks to decide the value of security dependent on showcase results, for example, income and benefits, the exploration or cost and volume are the subject of the specialized investigation. Specialized, diagnostic devices are utilized to inspect manners by which gracefully and interest for security will influence value, volume, and suggested unpredictability changes. Specialized examination is, for the most part, used to deliver momentary exchanging signals from different graphing techniques.

In any case, it can help improve the estimation of the power or shortcoming of security comparative with the more extensive market. This information permits experts to help the general assessment of the valuation there.

Recorded exchanging information can be utilized for specialized examination of any guard. This incorporates options, fates, products, monetary standards, fixed pay, and different protections. We will, as a rule, break down stocks in our models, however, recall that these ideas can be applied to pretty much every sort of insurance. Additionally, in products and forex markets, where merchants focus on transient value changes, the specialized examination is substantially more common.

The specialized examination tries to figure the value development of for all intents and purposes any tradable instrument commonly subject to flexibly and request powers, including stocks, bonds, prospects, and cash sets. Likewise, some view specialized investigates as simply watching the powers of flexibly and request as communicated in a security's market value developments. Specialized examination most as often as possible applies to value changes, yet a few investigators track numbers other than unimportant costs, for example, volume exchanging or figures of open premium.

There are several patterns and signals around the business that analysts have worked to help the specialized exchange examination. Specialized investigators additionally built up various kinds of exchanging frameworks to assist them with gauging value developments and exchange.

A few measurements center basically around distinguishing current patterns in the business, including regions of help and opposition. Interestingly, others focus on surveying the force of a pattern and the likelihood of its duration.

Regularly utilized specialized pointers and examples for outlining incorporate trend lines, channels, moving midpoints, and indications of force.

Specialized experts normally take a gander at the accompanying expansive sorts of markers:

- Market developments
- Chart volume and force markers
- Oscillators
- Moving midpoints
- Support and obstruction rates

Specialized examination differs from the basic investigation in that the main sources of info are the cost and volume of the stock. The focal supposition that will be that every single realized key is considered into the expense; thus, they don't should be given close consideration. Specialized examiners are not endeavoring to ascertain the inherent estimation of an item. In any case, they are rather utilizing stock diagrams to distinguish examples and patterns that demonstrate what a stock will do later on.

Chapter 5: Strategies for Options Trading

At the point when you handle the essentials of exchanging options, you're ready to get the show on the road.

Exchanging options run a hazard. The most significant thing, however, is understanding what you're doing. Warren Buffet stated, "Hazard is the place you don't have the foggiest idea what you're doing." There'll consistently be a hazard in exchanging and contributing; what you have to recollect is to have a brighter view of what you're doing. The way to noteworthy and steady advantage in exchanging options is to build up an effective exchanging system and afterward make a progression of methodologies that will assist you with accomplishing your objectives.

With regard to exchanging options, many individuals simply talk about putting and calling shares. All things considered, that is the start. You should gain proficiency with the rudiments of the exchange. From that point, you need to take a gander at a portion of the methodologies that will permit you to do well in the exchange. We will take a gander at steps and methodologies dependent on your exchanging plan to guarantee you are doing admirably in options exchanging.

5.1 Long Call/ Long Put (Going Long Strategies)

Options are part of the alternative's "call" and "put." With a call choice, the agreement holder secures the option to buy the hidden resource at a fixed cost, later on, called the activity cost or the strike cost. With a put alternative, the purchaser gets the right to sell the fundamental resource at the concurred cost later on.

Long Call Technique

Options are utilized instruments, i.e., by giving up littler sums than would somehow or another be required when selling the hidden resource itself, they empower merchants to boost the benefit. An ordinary investment opportunity contract controls 100 basic security shares.

Assume a dealer needs to purchase Apple (AAPL) stocks, $165 an offer. With that value, the individual in question can purchase 30 offers for $4,950. At that point, envision the stock value ascends by 10 percent throughout the following month to $181.50. Disregarding any exchanging, commission, or exchange costs, the broker's portfolio would develop to $5,445, leaving the merchant with a net profit for the cash contributed of $495, or 10 percent.

Assume a call choice on a similar stock, with a $165 strike value that will terminate about a month from now cost $5.50 per share or $550 per contract. Given the speculation spending plan accessible to the financial specialist, the individual in question can buy nine options at the expense of $4,950. Since the alternative agreement oversees 100 offers, the dealer makes an arrangement on 900 offers successfully. In the event that the stock value ascends at expiry by 10 percent to $181.50, the choice lapses in the cash and is worth $16.50 per share ($181.50-$165 strikes), or $14,850 on the 900 offers. That is a net dollar return of nearly $9,990, or 200 percent on the put-away cash, a lot better yield contrasted with direct exchanging of the hidden resource. (See "Does a financial specialist hold or exercise choice?" for applicable perusing)

The merchant's conceivable misfortune from a long call is confined to the superior payable. The potential advantage is boundless in light of the fact that the payout choice will ascend before expiry alongside the hidden resource cost, and actually, there is no restriction on how high it can go.

It is the picked system for merchants who are bullish or hopeful about a particular stock, ETF, or list and needs to lessen the hazard.

Long Put Technique

A put choice works similarly in which a call choice does, with the put choice expanding enthusiasm as the hidden value diminishes. Albeit short-selling regularly permits a dealer to profit by falling costs; the short-situated hazard is unending. For a put alternative, the choice will lapse uselessly if the fundamental falls over the strike cost of the agreement.

Conceivable hazard for options is constrained to the premium charged. As the hidden cost can't dip under zero, the likely profit by the agreement is topped, similarly likewise with a long call choice, the put alternative to use the arrival of the financial specialist.

5.2 Long/Short (Strangles and Straddles)

Strangle and Straddle are the two options exchanging methodologies that permit the financial specialist to exploit noteworthy varieties in the cost of a stock, regardless of whether the stock goes up or down. The two methodologies incorporate purchasing an equivalent number of calls and put options with a similar expiry date.

Strangle

The strangle exchange is one way a dealer can profit by a basic resource's value change. Suppose an enterprise is planned to report its present outcomes in three weeks. Such weeks before the news discharge will be a magnificent opportunity to join strangle since the stock is probably going to move drastically, sequentially, when the outcomes are discharged.

Suppose that in April, the stock exchanges at $15. Assume a June call alternative of $15 has a cost of $2, while the June call choice of $15 put is $1. Purchasing both the call and the put for an aggregate sum of $300: $3 x 100 offers for each agreement choice = $300 finishes a ride.

In the events that the stock moves higher goes lower, the ride will ascend in esteem. Benefits can be acknowledged, as long as the stock value ascends toward any path by more than $3 per share.

Straddle

Straddle position is another answer for options. Albeit a strangle has no directional inclination, a straddle is utilized when the speculator expects that the stock has a higher possibility of heading a particular way; however, it might likewise want to be on the protected edge in case of a troublesome change.

We should accept you accept, for example, that the consequences of business would be acceptable, which means you need less protection against the drawback. Rather than buying the put choice with the $15 strike cost for $1, perhaps you're taking a gander at buying the $12.50 strike that has a $0.25 reward. This trade would cost not exactly the ride, and would likewise permit you to part even less of an upward push.

Utilizing the choice to put the lower strike in this choke would, in any case, shield you from a huge drawback, therefore placing you in a more grounded position to profit by a triumphant declaration also.

5.3 Iron Condor

At the point when you purchase an iron condor, it's your expectation that from the second you open the situation until the options terminate, the basic file or security will remain inside a sensibly limited exchanging range. When termination shows up, if all options are out of worth, they lapse uselessly, and you have each penny (fewer commissions) you gain once you purchase the iron condor. Try not to anticipate that the ideal situation should happen inevitably, yet it will occur. Frequently giving up the last hardly any nickels or dimes of future payments is best, and shutting the spot before the termination date shows up. This permits the broker to secure a decent benefit and evacuates the opportunity of disappointment. Hazard the board limit is basic expertise for all merchants, particularly those utilizing this procedure.

The business sectors are not generally that benevolent, and basic file or stock qualities can be unusual. The fundamental resource (XYZ or ABCD in past models) can experience a noteworthy value change when that occurs. Since that is bad for your place (or wallet), you need to think about two vital snippets of data: the amount you can lose; and what you ought to do when the market is wrong.

5.4 Iron Butterfly

An iron butterfly is an exchanging alternative that utilizes four separate agreements as a major aspect of a technique to exploit stocks or fates costs falling inside a given range. Trade is regularly intended to profit by an abatement in inferred unpredictability. The secret to utilizing this exchange as a major aspect of a beneficial exchanging plan is envisioning a period when alternative costs are probably going to diminish in esteem commonly.

This normally occurs during times of sidelong development, or a slight upward pattern. The exchange is additionally known under the epithet "Iron Fly."

The Iron Butterfly exchange is made with four options comprising of two options to call and two options to put. Such calls and puts are appropriated more than three-strike rates, all of which have a similar expiry date. The point is to profit by circumstances under which the value remains generally consistent, and the options show a suggested decrease and chronicled instability.

It can likewise be viewed as a half and half choice exchange utilizing both a short ride and a long choke, with the ride situated in the focal point of the three strike costs and the straddles put above and beneath the middle strike cost on two extra strikes.

Exchange picks up the full advantage when at the end of the expiry, the fundamental resource closes definitely on the center strike point.

5.5 Equity Collar

In money, the term neckline normally alludes to a strategy for chance administration, called a guarded neckline. The utilization of collars is less plugged for different cases. Be that as this may, with a little exertion and information, dealers can utilize the guideline of the neckline to oversee chance, and now and again, increment the pace of benefit. A neckline is an options exchanging technique created by holding portions of the fundamental stock while buying guarded puts simultaneously and selling call options against that holding. The puts and gets are both out-of-the-cash options having exactly the same lapse date month, and the number of agreements must rise to. This article analyzes how strategies for neckline resistance and bullishness work.

This strategy is additionally utilized in the utilization of file options to insure against the chance of misfortune on a long stock or an entire value portfolio. This can likewise be utilized with the utilization of roofs and floors to moderate financing cost variances for the two speculators and loan specialists.

Defensive collars are viewed as a strategy that is bearish to unbiased. Similarly, as with the upside, the misfortune in a defensive neckline is negligible.

Call options offer financial specialists the right; however, not the obligation, to purchase the stock at the value set, called the strike cost. Put options offer financial specialists the option to sell the stock at the strike cost yet not the obligation. The superior, which is the expense of the call options, is added to the put purchase, in this manner diminishing the general premium charged for the position. This system is suggested after a period where the offer cost of stock has ascended, as it is planned to protect benefits as opposed to raise returns.

5.6 Short Gut

The short gut is an options exchanging strategy that is utilized to deliver a net benefit when the security value remains inside characterized limits for a given period. It's very near both the short ride and the short choke, yet the short gut will deliver benefits from a more extensive value run than both.

Nonetheless, on the other hand, the potential upgrades that can be made are lower. This strategy incorporates composing offers for getting an underlying advance, with the desire that every potential venture would be not as much as that advance. On the off chance that the fundamental security cost should rise essentially past as far as possible, at that point, the potential misfortunes can be noteworthy.

In this way, this is a strategy that requires cautious thought. The short gut is proposed to be utilized when your security standpoint is sensibly nonpartisan; however, you need to permit some development in either course. Except if the security moves altogether toward any path, the potential misfortunes are boundless, so you should be certain that such a move is unthinkable before utilizing this strategy.

A credit spread is made; however, there is consistently a requirement for edge since you have to have enough venture capital. You will require a serious extent of exchanging with your merchant, as well.

To execute a Short Gut, you have to situate two deals simultaneously as your merchant to open requests. You have to compose dependent on the pivotal insurance in the cash call options and compose a proportional number in the cash calls. The agreement expiry date will be the equivalent, and it very well may be as long haul or as the present moment as you wish.

A momentary lapse date implies less an ideal opportunity to change in cost for the fundamental security; however, there is the less outward incentive for transient options. Benefits are produced using the expanding options' extraneous worth, so less outward worth would approach less future advantage. Longer-term agreements may convey more as far as future advantages, yet they set aside more effort at the security cost to change enough to deliver a misfortune.

The other choice that you need to make is how much the agreements you compose are in the bank. The calls and puts ought to be in cash by a proportional whole (i.e., the strikes ought to be equidistant from the exchanging stock's present selling cost), so you have to choose the amount you need the strikes from the current exchanging cost.

The further the options in the capital, the higher the value run from which you'll pick up. Nonetheless, as options move further in the market, the outward worth abatements and your potential advantage will be lower. Basically, the choice is whether to expand the odds of making a benefit or to build the size of the conceivable favorable position.

5.7 Long Gut

A long gut, or "gut spread," is an options system made by purchasing or selling an in-cash (ITM) that is assembled with an ITM call. Options dealers utilize enormous intestinal spreads in circumstances where they expect the basic stock will rise significantly however are uncertain with respect to whether it is going up or down. On the other hand, when the fundamental stock isn't required to roll out any recognizable improvement, a little gut spread is utilized.

A long gut remembers purchasing and putting a for the-cash request.

A long gut spread advantages if the hidden market makes a noteworthy value change before the options run out.

The short guts are an impartial options exchanging technique that includes all the while selling an in-the-cash call and placing in-the-cash of the equivalent hid stock and expiry date.

This is a restricted advantage, boundless hazard options exchanging system taken when the options merchant anticipates that in the close to term, the basic stock will experience little instability. The short guts are a credit spread since it assumes a net acknowledgment to enter the trade.

Chapter 6: Setting up for the Ultimate Success

Options are one of the most adaptable monetary market instruments. Their adaptability uses the merchant's situation to raise returns. These items frequently permit the purchaser to oversee chance by utilizing them to support or to make a benefit from the market's upside, drawback, and sideways developments.

In spite of its numerous focal points, exchanging options conveys a significant danger of misfortune and is theoretical. Not every person can form into a fruitful dealer of options. Likewise, with some other organization, being a decent dealer of options requires a specific arrangement of abilities, character style, and disposition.

6.1 The Trader's Mindset

Value exchanging is about the objectives for quality, stop-misfortune, and benefit. Exchanging options are around a time span and openings spaces. Forty-five days and a $150-$190 value go; for instance.

Your consideration is on your entrance cost and your Profit and Loss when you start another value exchange. You've founded on static focuses and an obscure chance to manufacture an increase or burden for the Exchange. "Invalid and dubious" leaves no space for feeling fidgety about the outcome.

Here's the distinction, from the beginning, options exchanges are based on knowing how the consummation looks and how long you need to arrive at the point.

Also, it's improving. Most options merchants have a lucky opening to bring in cash in an arrangement, and a few events to gain a benefit. You just make a directional call while you're managing values. This is it. One situation makes a benefit, and just a single situation does.

Discover procedures that you can surely know. Use them when you think economic situations are sensible (i.e., secured call composing and stripped put selling function admirably in a somewhat bullish condition; iron condors work well when advertise instability is high yet gradually declining).

Discover how well you expected the business condition to turn into a reality. After some time, you'll make sense of which approaches perform well — not just in light of the fact that the procedure itself was practical — yet more critically, in light of the fact that you've executed it at the correct second.

Create discipline with the goal that unavoidable misfortune can be taken.

Know when it is sufficient, and leave winning exchanges when the staying conceivable advantage is too low to even think about warranting the danger of getting the keep going barely any nickels on an agreement.

6.2 Keeping a Trading Journal

Exchanging diaries assist brokers with monitoring their exchanges and contemplations throughout the day. It is an awesome apparatus in light of the fact that your business explanation contains data past what you can discover in an itemized article. It incorporates what economic situations have been similar to and whether you have been occupied or committed errors. It's likewise where you can record thoughts for a system that may come up as your Exchange for the duration of the day.

All brokers should keep an exchanging log; however, there is no ideal opportunity for informal investors to hold nothing back the entire day on paper. Holding an exchanging diary when exchanging — while the move is taking place — may conceivably be counter-beneficial and bring about missed exchanges.

In any case, there's a simple arrangement that requires definitely no penmanship and gives you a verifiable record of the specific economic situations you looked on a given day.

For the duration of the day, most merchants mark their graphs, drawing lines, and stamping marker rates that help decide the pattern and discover conceivable inversion/target focuses. The chart shows the specific exchanging conditions in the market. Intraday will show your perspective available that day — something words would never clarify in an exchanging diary also.

An image is a simple method to keep an exchanging diary, yet when you glance back at it for a survey, you should incorporate certain things that make it helpful. Think back to perceive what you did toward the finish of every week to a month, note regular issues, and recognize your qualities. Such bits of knowledge will assist you with exploiting your qualities and show the territories where you have to improve.

Screen captures are more productive at gathering data than simply writing in a diary could. In addition, you can do it directly on your diagrams in the event that you need to record things, or you can even keep a composed exchanging log.

6.3 Buying and Selling Calls as a Learning Opportunity

A call alternative by and large alluded to as a "call," is a sort of a subordinates contract that gives the speculator the right, however not the commitment, to buy a stock or some other money-related instrument at a particular value, the choice's strike cost – inside a given time period. The alternative dealer is committed to offering the security to the buyer if the last needs to utilize their entitlement to make a buy. The alternative holder may practice the choice whenever before the determined expiry date. Later on, the expiry date perhaps three months, a half year, or even a year. The merchant gets the price tag for the choice, which depends on how close the alternative strike value is to the basic security cost at the time the choice is bought, and how long a period stays until the expiry date of choice. At the end of the day, the choice's cost depends on how likely, or far-fetched, the alternative purchaser will be allowed to practice the choice beneficially before expiry. Options are normally sold in loads of 100 offers.

The purchaser of an alternative call means to make a benefit if and when the cost of the fundamental resource increments to a level more huge than the degree of the choice strike. Then again, the call alternative dealer trusts the advantage's cost will fall, or if nothing else increments as high as the strike/practice value an incentive until it lapses, in which case the cash earned for selling the sum will be a genuine advantage.

In the event that the cost of the security doesn't transcend the strike cost until expiry, at that point, the alternative won't be valuable for the financial specialist to practice the right, and the correct will terminate uselessly or "out of the pocket."

The client endures a misfortune equivalent to the cost of the call choice, in the event that the cost of the particular security increments over the cost of the alternative strike, the financial specialist may practice this choice productively.

For instance, expect you've bought an alternative on 100 stock offers, with a $30 strike cost. Before your choice runs out, the stock value ascends from $28 to $40. You could then exercise your entitlement to purchase 100 stock offers at $30, giving you a moment of $10 per share advantage. Your net benefit will be 100 offers, $10 times an offer, short any price tag you paid for the choice. In the event that you paid $200 for the call choice in this model, at that point, your net benefit would add up to $800 (100 offers x $10 per share-$ 200 = $800).

Purchasing call options permits speculators to spend a limited quantity of funding to profit by a cost increment in the fundamental security possibly, or to support away from the positional dangers. Little speculators use options to transform little wholes of capital into critical benefits, while corporate and institutional financial specialists use options to raise their minor profit and support their value portfolios.

Purchasing a Call Choice

The purchaser is alluded to as the holder of a call choice. The purchaser purchases a call alternative trusting the cost will increment over the strike cost and before the expiry date. The benefit earned is equivalent to the returns of the deal, less the expense of the strike, the premium, and any conditional charges related to the deal.

On the off chances that the cost doesn't transcend the strike value, the correct won't be practiced by the purchaser.

The purchaser will be managed a misfortune equivalent to the call alternative premium. For instance, accept the supply of ABC Company is selling at $40, and an alternative call agreement is estimated at $2 with a strike cost of $40 and a one-month expiry.

With a strike cost of $40, the financial specialist is confident that the stock cost will rise and pay $200 for one ABC call choice. On the off chance that ABC's stock increments from $40 to $50, the purchaser will acquire $1000 in net pay and $800 in a net benefit.

Selling a Call Choice

Call choice sellers, otherwise called creators, offer to consider options in the desire that at the expiry date, they will get useless. They bring in cash by stashing the premiums (costs) they have been paying. Their benefit will be scaled down, or even an overall deficit, if the choice purchaser practices its alternative productively when the security value ascends over the choice strike cost.

6.4 Types of Trading

There are numerous sorts of options that can be exchanged, and in various ways, these can be arranged. There are two chief structures, from a specific perspective: calls and puts. Considers giving the purchaser the option to buy the basic resource, in this manner selling the hidden resource gives the purchaser the right. Alongside this generous differentiation, options are regularly frequently evaluated by whether they are American or European style. This has nothing to do with the topographical area, yet rather with the activity of the agreements. Get familiar with the varieties underneath.

Options might be additionally characterized dependent on the framework in which they are traded, their time of expiry, and the fundamental security to which they contribute. Other explicit sorts and a few colorful options exist, as well.

Calls

Call options are gets that permit the proprietor to purchase the basic resource at a concurred cost later on. On the off chances that you accept that the hidden resource was probably going to ascend in cost over a given timeframe, you will purchase a call. Calls have an expiry date, and the basic resource can be bought whenever before the expiry date or at the expiry date, contingent upon the provisions of the agreement. If it's not too much trouble, visit the accompanying connection Calls for increasingly explicit data on this sort and a few models.

Puts

Setting options are basically something contrary to calls. The proprietor of a put will reserve the option to sell the hidden resource at a fixed cost later on. What's more, in the event that you were anticipating that the hidden resource should fall in esteem, you should purchase a put. There is an expiry date in the contact for calls. It would be ideal if you read the accompanying article – Puts – for extra subtleties and instances of how puts options work.

American Style

As respects options, the expression "American style" has nothing to do with where agreements are bought or sold, yet rather with the terms of agreements. Agreements for options accompany an expiry date, at which stage the buyer has the privilege to buy or sell the fundamental security (if a call) (if a put). With American-style options, the agreement proprietor additionally has the privilege to practice before the expiry date whenever. This additional flexibility speaks to a huge advantage for an American-style contract proprietor. You can discover more data on the accompanying page-American Style Options and working models.

European Style

The proprietors of agreements with European style options are not given similar adaptability likewise with contracts in the American style. On the off chances that you own an agreement in European style, at that point, you are qualified to buy or sell the fundamental resource on which the agreement depends on the expiry date and not previously. For more data on this sort of European Style Options, it would be ideal if you read the accompanying article.

Exchange-Traded Options

The expression "Traded" is utilized to portray any agreement options which are recorded on a stock trade. They can be bought and sold by anybody utilizing a legitimate merchant's administrations.

Over the Counter Options

"Over the Counter" (OTC) options are exchanged just the OTC markets, making them less openly accessible. They will, in general, be more entangled than most Exchange Traded contracts, with altered agreements.

6.5 Risk Management

Numerous individuals mistakenly presume that options are regularly more dangerous ventures than stocks since they don't totally see precisely what options are and how they work. Without a doubt, options can be utilized to fence positions and decrease chance, for instance, with a cautious put. Options may likewise be utilized to wager on a stock going up or down yet with considerably less hazard than purchasing or shortening the fundamental stock's genuine partner. This last utilization of hazard minimization options in making directional wagers will be the subject of this subchapter.

Traditional Risk Calculation

The typical and most normal way is the main strategy for adjusting hazard uniqueness. We should return to our model and perceive how this functions: If you'd put $10,000 in a $50 stock, you'd get 200 offers. You could likewise purchase two separate call choice agreements, rather than purchasing the 200 offers. By buying the options, you pay less cash yet, at the same time, have a similar number of offers under administration. The quantity of options is assessed by the number of offers that the venture capital could have purchased.

Let's assume you intend to purchase 1,000 XYZ shares at $4175 for a $41.750 all-out expense. Notwithstanding, rather than purchasing the stock at $4175, you can pay $1.630 per contract for ten alternative call agreements whose strike cost is $30 (in-the-cash). The buying options would bring about a gross cost of $16.300 in the capital for the ten calls. That is a net investment fund of $25450, or around 60 percent of what you'd spend on buying the offers.

That reserve funds of $25.450 can be utilized in an assortment of ways. Right off the bat, it can make the most of different chances to offer you more expansion. Second, it can just protest an exchanging record and increase costs on the currency advertise. Intrigue accumulation may set up what is known as a manufactured profit. For instance, if the $25.450 reserve funds in a currency advertise account increases 2 percent intrigue for each year. The record will get $509 intrigue a year over the existence time of the agreement, which is equal to about $42 per month.

As it were, you are presently acquiring a profit on a stock that doesn't pay one while as yet benefitting from the offer of options. Likewise, this can be cultivated, utilizing about 33% of the assets expected to purchase the stock straightforwardly.

Elective Hazard Count

The other hazard-based option for adjusting cost and size divergence.

Purchasing $10,000 in stock isn't equivalent to purchasing $10,000 in all-out hazard options, as we have found. Presentation options convey a lot of higher hazard because of extensively expanded misfortune potential. You should have a hazard proportional options position with respect to the stock situation to even the odds.

How about we start with stock position: purchasing 1,000 offers for an all-out venture of $41.750, at $41.75. Being a cognizant hazard speculator, you are additionally entering a stop-misfortune request, a judicious system that showcase specialists exhort.

You set a stop request at a cost, confining your misfortune to 20 percent of the speculation, which is $8.350.

On the off chances that this is the sum, you're willing to lose, the sum you're prepared to pay on an options job will likewise be the sum. In the long run, you can just burn through $8,350 on hazard identicalness buy options. With this procedure, you are in the situation of options with a similar dollar sum in danger as you were eager to lose in-stock position.

Stop orders won't shield you from whole openings in the event that you own stock. For an options contract, if the stock opens underneath the strike cost, you've lost all that you may lose, which is the aggregate sum of cash you spent purchasing the calls. You may endure a considerably more critical misfortune on the off chance that you own the stock with the goal that the situation of the options turns out to be less unsafe than the situation of the stock.

Let's assume you are purchasing a $60 biotech stock, and it holes down at $20 when a test quiet is murdered by the organization's medication. Your stop request will be executed at $20, securing a deplorable loss of $40. In this circumstance, your stop request was not bearing a lot of security.

State, however, you pass on stock possession and buy the call options for $11.50. Your hazard circumstance is presently moving radically, as just the measure of cash you paid for the alternative is in danger. Also, if the stock opens at $20, your mates who purchased the stock will be down $40, while you will lose $11.50. At the point when utilized along these lines, the options are less dangerous than the stocks.

Conclusion

In the wake of following this book, you more likely than not made sense of how simple options trading is. With the data secured here and your craving to make it in options trading, you have no alternative yet to exceed expectations in the business. You are currently more ready to trade options utilizing specialized examination, crucial investigation, and different techniques. You are additionally prepared to accept open astoundingly and know what each exchange involves, from a dedicated view.

- Calls give you the option to buy an advantage while puts permit you to sell a profit.
- A choice alludes to an agreement that gives a purchaser the position to purchase or sell an advantage at a specific cost inside a particular period.
- The expense of an alternative is alluded to as the premium.
- Options don't speak to the genuine estimation of power or fundamental security. An alternative in itself is a subsidiary of a benefit or security
- Long-term options are otherwise called jumps
- The options advertise has four members. These are the purchaser of a call, the purchaser of a put, the merchant of a call, and the vender of a put.

At this point, you comprehend that there are a decent number of devices and stages that you can use to trade options. Since the expense of options continues fluctuating from the beginning date to the development date, you need a step that best suits your exchanging and preparing needs.

Remember that every action has its qualities and shortcomings; in this manner, you may not discover one that is 100 percent viable.

A decent stage is one that enables you to tailor your experience. Such a step can oblige both beginner and experienced brokers. An advanced stage can contrarily affect your capability since you will invest a lot of energy attempting to comprehend the propelled devices and highlights on the step. Having the correct instrument will guarantee that you exchange with certainty.

We were unable to end the conversation without referencing monetary influence as an advantage of exchanging options. The impact comes about when you can interpret your little capital into gigantic additions. It emerges from how a rate increment in the cost of an alternative is generally higher than the expansion in the primary resource. This implies the more you contribute, the higher the money related influence. With a decent exchanging arrangement, you can utilize this idea to limit exchanging dangers and amplify your profits. An extraordinary bit of leeway in options trading is that the options contract itself is now an influence opportunity. It permits you to become your beginning capital without any problem. At this point, you ought to have the option to compute the influence of some random position utilizing the delta esteem.

With regards to options trading, persistence and duty are critical. It would help if you had the power to control your feelings. Passionate exchanging is a hazardous issue. Rewarding options like some other business can help oversee misfortunes effortlessly. Making exchanges since they appear to be acceptable can lead you into inconvenience.

In reality, the distinction between great brokers and normal ones is that a decent merchant doesn't permit feelings to control him.

When he loses, he comprehends that it is because he settled on an off-base move or decision and that it isn't the framework that is neutralizing him. Great merchants don't plunge into superfluous open doors as a result of emotions; they weigh the options and settle on choices dependent on what is exchanged for them. They likewise comprehend when to stop trade regardless of whether a few misfortunes are caused.

Likewise, we took a gander at a portion of the tips you have to utilize to guarantee that you prevail in the majority of your exchanges, if not all. These are basic things, such as gathering enough capital before you begin trading, distinguishing a reasonable exchanging style, and having a hazard the executives plan. Moreover, you have known a bit of the slip-up most vendors make when exchanging options and how you can keep up a critical right way from them.

With this knowledge into the options showcase, you ought to have the option to do an exchange all the way, effectively. You should, in any case, note that the options business isn't for each speculator. It can get advanced and risky if you don't incorporate the data plot in this book.

At this point, it is evident to you whether this is a venture you need to give it a shot or not. If you are into it, you should choose the sort of merchant you would need to be. You can either be an informal investor, a long-haul broker, or a momentary merchant. As a casual investor, you will have the upside of making a few exchanges that nearby rapidly. This choice is beneficial for you on the off chance that you are keen on making little benefits. Something else, consider long haul exchanging that can traverse a time of more than 30 days, however, with mind-blowing benefits.

Exchanging on options likewise includes picking the fundamental security that you would wish to interface your options too.

This might be as wares, stock, or foreign money. Every cash has its attributes, and the liquidity status additionally matters. Wares are acceptable yet unpredictable, monetary forms exchange more often than not, yet the costs are effortlessly affected by financial news things. Stocks experience a fast change in prices for the time being.

To numerous individuals, options are a convoluted instrument to exchange. In any case, the more you get some answers concerning them, the less distressing they become. With some experience, you understand that the instrument is one of the most adaptable to exchange. In any case, for options trading to work out in the right way, you additionally need to comprehend the rudiments of picking a stock, surveying market cycles, and defining venture techniques.

Since options are profoundly unpredictable, on the off chance that you don't practice alert, you may lose all your speculation at one go. That is the reason you need particular preparation, for example, this one preceding wandering into it. A decent number of individuals that have to prevail in options exchanging started as stockbrokers. If you are as of now into the stock exchange, you will have simple time transferring options because of the numerous similitudes that exist between the two.

In conclusion, note that the shorter the exchanging time frame, the higher the pressure and dangers included. If you continue holding your exchanges as the night progresses, you stand a high risk of losing your capital and pulverizing your record. Other than this, we are happy that you have taken in another method of gaining cash from the money related market and saw all the qualities and abilities you have to make it in parallel options exchanging. Note that the hypothesis is never influential without training.

With these lines, if you need to start, it is perfect for perceiving a trading stage and setting up what you have acknowledged as an ordinary event. Continuously Keep this at the top of the priority list that the more you practice it, the more sure you become.

www.ingramcontent.com/pod-product-compliance
Lightning Source LLC
Chambersburg PA
CBHW051537240526
45465CB00027B/598